C-4378   CAREER EXAMINATION SERIES

This is your
PASSBOOK for...

Library Clerk II

Test Preparation Study Guide
Questions & Answers

COPYRIGHT NOTICE

This book is SOLELY intended for, is sold ONLY to, and its use is RESTRICTED to individual, bona fide applicants or candidates who qualify by virtue of having seriously filed applications for appropriate license, certificate, professional and/or promotional advancement, higher school matriculation, scholarship, or other legitimate requirements of education and/or governmental authorities.

This book is NOT intended for use, class instruction, tutoring, training, duplication, copying, reprinting, excerption, or adaptation, etc., by:

1) Other publishers
2) Proprietors and/or Instructors of "Coaching" and/or Preparatory Courses
3) Personnel and/or Training Divisions of commercial, industrial, and governmental organizations
4) Schools, colleges, or universities and/or their departments and staffs, including teachers and other personnel
5) Testing Agencies or Bureaus
6) Study groups which seek by the purchase of a single volume to copy and/or duplicate and/or adapt this material for use by the group as a whole without having purchased individual volumes for each of the members of the group
7) Et al.

Such persons would be in violation of appropriate Federal and State statutes.

PROVISION OF LICENSING AGREEMENTS – Recognized educational, commercial, industrial, and governmental institutions and organizations, and others legitimately engaged in educational pursuits, including training, testing, and measurement activities, may address request for a licensing agreement to the copyright owners, who will determine whether, and under what conditions, including fees and charges, the materials in this book may be used them. In other words, a licensing facility exists for the legitimate use of the material in this book on other than an individual basis. However, it is asseverated and affirmed here that the material in this book CANNOT be used without the receipt of the express permission of such a licensing agreement from the Publishers. Inquiries re licensing should be addressed to the company, attention rights and permissions department.

All rights reserved, including the right of reproduction in whole or in part, in any form or by any means, electronic or mechanical, including photocopying, recording, or by any information storage and retrieval system, without permission in writing from the Publisher.

Copyright © 2025 by
National Learning Corporation

212 Michael Drive, Syosset, NY 11791
(516) 921-8888 • www.passbooks.com
E-mail: info@passbooks.com

PASSBOOK® SERIES

THE *PASSBOOK® SERIES* has been created to prepare applicants and candidates for the ultimate academic battlefield – the examination room.

At some time in our lives, each and every one of us may be required to take an examination – for validation, matriculation, admission, qualification, registration, certification, or licensure.

Based on the assumption that every applicant or candidate has met the basic formal educational standards, has taken the required number of courses, and read the necessary texts, the *PASSBOOK® SERIES* furnishes the one special preparation which may assure passing with confidence, instead of failing with insecurity. Examination questions – together with answers – are furnished as the basic vehicle for study so that the mysteries of the examination and its compounding difficulties may be eliminated or diminished by a sure method.

This book is meant to help you pass your examination provided that you qualify and are serious in your objective.

The entire field is reviewed through the huge store of content information which is succinctly presented through a provocative and challenging approach – the question-and-answer method.

A climate of success is established by furnishing the correct answers at the end of each test.

You soon learn to recognize types of questions, forms of questions, and patterns of questioning. You may even begin to anticipate expected outcomes.

You perceive that many questions are repeated or adapted so that you can gain acute insights, which may enable you to score many sure points.

You learn how to confront new questions, or types of questions, and to attack them confidently and work out the correct answers.

You note objectives and emphases, and recognize pitfalls and dangers, so that you may make positive educational adjustments.

Moreover, you are kept fully informed in relation to new concepts, methods, practices, and directions in the field.

You discover that you are actually taking the examination all the time: you are preparing for the examination by "taking" an examination, not by reading extraneous and/or supererogatory textbooks.

In short, this PASSBOOK®, used directedly, should be an important factor in helping you to pass your test.

LIBRARY CLERK II

DUTIES:
Performs clerical duties in a public library and assists library patrons in using the materials and equipment in the library. Arranges or files materials according to library filing rules. Performs routine searches of and updates to computer records. Issues borrowers cards according to library procedures. Performs routine circulation, reserve and overdue functions. Makes and checks routine arithmetic computations. Answers the telephone and takes messages. Calls patrons to deliver messages or information on library materials. Types cards, lists, labels, or short entries on forms. Assists a librarian in charging and discharging books, registering borrowers, collecting fines, reserving books and answering routine questions concerning the library's collections and services while working at the circulation and reference desks. Prepares overdue notices and catalog cards; files shelf list cards; oversees and revises the pasting and lettering of new books; prepares books and magazines for the bindery. Maintains records and assists in the preparation of bills, purchase orders, payrolls and statistical reports for the main and branch libraries. Performs related work as required.

As a Library Clerk II, you would engage in specialized library clerical activities in support of a library program, such as organizing and maintaining the library collection, helping library patrons locate information, maintaining online databases, acquiring library materials, processing library materials using an integrated library system (ILS), and shelving and rebinding books. You may have responsibilities in one or more organizational units within the library, such as Reference, Circulation, Interlibrary Loan, Special Collections, Periodicals, Acquisitions, Government Documents, Preservation, Digitization or Cataloging. You may be called upon to supervise library para professionals, technical support staff, student workers, interns, or volunteers. If you are assigned to a Department of Corrections and Community Supervision facility you may supervise inmate library clerks.

SCOPE OF THE EXAMINATION:
The written test will be designed to test for knowledge, skills and/or abilities in such areas as:
1. **Fundamentals of working in a library** - These questions are designed to evaluate the candidate's knowledge about the common terms and concepts used in various sections of a library (e.g. circulation, reference, technical processing, etc.); the procedures associated with shelving, storing, checking out and receiving library materials; and the proper methods of using equipment commonly found in a library and of handling, processing and storing library materials.
2. **Name and number checking** - These questions test for the ability to distinguish between sets of words, letters, and/or numbers that are almost exactly alike. Material is usually presented in two or three columns, and you will have to determine how the entry in the first column compares with the entry in the second column and possibly the third. You will be instructed to mark your answers according to a designated code provided in the directions.
3. **Office record keeping** - These questions test your ability to perform common office record keeping tasks. The test consists of two or more "sets" of questions, each set concerning a different problem. Typical record keeping problems might involve the organization or collation of data from several sources; scheduling; maintaining a record system using running balances; or completion of a table summarizing data using totals, subtotals, averages and percents.
4. **Public contact principles and practices** - These questions test for knowledge of techniques used to interact with other people, to gather and present information, and to provide assistance, advice, and effective customer service in a courteous and professional manner. Questions will cover such topics as understanding and responding to people with diverse needs, perspectives, personalities, and levels of familiarity with agency operations, as well as acting in a way that both serves the public and reflects well on your agency.
5. **Understanding and interpreting written material** - These questions test for the ability to understand and interpret written material. You will be presented with brief reading passages and will be asked questions about the passages. You should base your answers to the questions only on what is presented in the passages and not on what you may happen to know about the topic.

HOW TO TAKE A TEST

I. YOU MUST PASS AN EXAMINATION

A. *WHAT EVERY CANDIDATE SHOULD KNOW*

Examination applicants often ask us for help in preparing for the written test. What can I study in advance? What kinds of questions will be asked? How will the test be given? How will the papers be graded?

As an applicant for a civil service examination, you may be wondering about some of these things. Our purpose here is to suggest effective methods of advance study and to describe civil service examinations.

Your chances for success on this examination can be increased if you know how to prepare. Those "pre-examination jitters" can be reduced if you know what to expect. You can even experience an adventure in good citizenship if you know why civil service exams are given.

B. *WHY ARE CIVIL SERVICE EXAMINATIONS GIVEN?*

Civil service examinations are important to you in two ways. As a citizen, you want public jobs filled by employees who know how to do their work. As a job seeker, you want a fair chance to compete for that job on an equal footing with other candidates. The best-known means of accomplishing this two-fold goal is the competitive examination.

Exams are widely publicized throughout the nation. They may be administered for jobs in federal, state, city, municipal, town or village governments or agencies.

Any citizen may apply, with some limitations, such as the age or residence of applicants. Your experience and education may be reviewed to see whether you meet the requirements for the particular examination. When these requirements exist, they are reasonable and applied consistently to all applicants. Thus, a competitive examination may cause you some uneasiness now, but it is your privilege and safeguard.

C. *HOW ARE CIVIL SERVICE EXAMS DEVELOPED?*

Examinations are carefully written by trained technicians who are specialists in the field known as "psychological measurement," in consultation with recognized authorities in the field of work that the test will cover. These experts recommend the subject matter areas or skills to be tested; only those knowledges or skills important to your success on the job are included. The most reliable books and source materials available are used as references. Together, the experts and technicians judge the difficulty level of the questions.

Test technicians know how to phrase questions so that the problem is clearly stated. Their ethics do not permit "trick" or "catch" questions. Questions may have been tried out on sample groups, or subjected to statistical analysis, to determine their usefulness.

Written tests are often used in combination with performance tests, ratings of training and experience, and oral interviews. All of these measures combine to form the best-known means of finding the right person for the right job.

II. HOW TO PASS THE WRITTEN TEST

A. NATURE OF THE EXAMINATION

To prepare intelligently for civil service examinations, you should know how they differ from school examinations you have taken. In school you were assigned certain definite pages to read or subjects to cover. The examination questions were quite detailed and usually emphasized memory. Civil service exams, on the other hand, try to discover your present ability to perform the duties of a position, plus your potentiality to learn these duties. In other words, a civil service exam attempts to predict how successful you will be. Questions cover such a broad area that they cannot be as minute and detailed as school exam questions.

In the public service similar kinds of work, or positions, are grouped together in one "class." This process is known as *position-classification*. All the positions in a class are paid according to the salary range for that class. One class title covers all of these positions, and they are all tested by the same examination.

B. FOUR BASIC STEPS

1) Study the announcement

How, then, can you know what subjects to study? Our best answer is: "Learn as much as possible about the class of positions for which you've applied." The exam will test the knowledge, skills and abilities needed to do the work.

Your most valuable source of information about the position you want is the official exam announcement. This announcement lists the training and experience qualifications. Check these standards and apply only if you come reasonably close to meeting them.

The brief description of the position in the examination announcement offers some clues to the subjects which will be tested. Think about the job itself. Review the duties in your mind. Can you perform them, or are there some in which you are rusty? Fill in the blank spots in your preparation.

Many jurisdictions preview the written test in the exam announcement by including a section called "Knowledge and Abilities Required," "Scope of the Examination," or some similar heading. Here you will find out specifically what fields will be tested.

2) Review your own background

Once you learn in general what the position is all about, and what you need to know to do the work, ask yourself which subjects you already know fairly well and which need improvement. You may wonder whether to concentrate on improving your strong areas or on building some background in your fields of weakness. When the announcement has specified "some knowledge" or "considerable knowledge," or has used adjectives like "beginning principles of…" or "advanced … methods," you can get a clue as to the number and difficulty of questions to be asked in any given field. More questions, and hence broader coverage, would be included for those subjects which are more important in the work. Now weigh your strengths and weaknesses against the job requirements and prepare accordingly.

3) Determine the level of the position

Another way to tell how intensively you should prepare is to understand the level of the job for which you are applying. Is it the entering level? In other words, is this the position in which beginners in a field of work are hired? Or is it an intermediate or advanced level? Sometimes this is indicated by such words as "Junior" or "Senior" in the class title. Other jurisdictions use Roman numerals to designate the level – Clerk I, Clerk II, for example. The word "Supervisor" sometimes appears in the title. If the level is not indicated by the title, check the description of duties. Will you be working under very close supervision, or will you have responsibility for independent decisions in this work?

4) Choose appropriate study materials

Now that you know the subjects to be examined and the relative amount of each subject to be covered, you can choose suitable study materials. For beginning level jobs, or even advanced ones, if you have a pronounced weakness in some aspect of your training, read a modern, standard textbook in that field. Be sure it is up to date and has general coverage. Such books are normally available at your library, and the librarian will be glad to help you locate one. For entry-level positions, questions of appropriate difficulty are chosen – neither highly advanced questions, nor those too simple. Such questions require careful thought but not advanced training.

If the position for which you are applying is technical or advanced, you will read more advanced, specialized material. If you are already familiar with the basic principles of your field, elementary textbooks would waste your time. Concentrate on advanced textbooks and technical periodicals. Think through the concepts and review difficult problems in your field.

These are all general sources. You can get more ideas on your own initiative, following these leads. For example, training manuals and publications of the government agency which employs workers in your field can be useful, particularly for technical and professional positions. A letter or visit to the government department involved may result in more specific study suggestions, and certainly will provide you with a more definite idea of the exact nature of the position you are seeking.

III. KINDS OF TESTS

Tests are used for purposes other than measuring knowledge and ability to perform specified duties. For some positions, it is equally important to test ability to make adjustments to new situations or to profit from training. In others, basic mental abilities not dependent on information are essential. Questions which test these things may not appear as pertinent to the duties of the position as those which test for knowledge and information. Yet they are often highly important parts of a fair examination. For very general questions, it is almost impossible to help you direct your study efforts. What we can do is to point out some of the more common of these general abilities needed in public service positions and describe some typical questions.

1) General information

Broad, general information has been found useful for predicting job success in some kinds of work. This is tested in a variety of ways, from vocabulary lists to questions about current events. Basic background in some field of work, such as sociology or economics, may be sampled in a group of questions. Often these are principles which have become familiar to most persons through exposure rather than through formal training. It is difficult to advise you how to study for these questions; being alert to the world around you is our best suggestion.

2) Verbal ability

An example of an ability needed in many positions is verbal or language ability. Verbal ability is, in brief, the ability to use and understand words. Vocabulary and grammar tests are typical measures of this ability. Reading comprehension or paragraph interpretation questions are common in many kinds of civil service tests. You are given a paragraph of written material and asked to find its central meaning.

3) Numerical ability

Number skills can be tested by the familiar arithmetic problem, by checking paired lists of numbers to see which are alike and which are different, or by interpreting charts and graphs. In the latter test, a graph may be printed in the test booklet which you are asked to use as the basis for answering questions.

4) Observation

A popular test for law-enforcement positions is the observation test. A picture is shown to you for several minutes, then taken away. Questions about the picture test your ability to observe both details and larger elements.

5) Following directions

In many positions in the public service, the employee must be able to carry out written instructions dependably and accurately. You may be given a chart with several columns, each column listing a variety of information. The questions require you to carry out directions involving the information given in the chart.

6) Skills and aptitudes

Performance tests effectively measure some manual skills and aptitudes. When the skill is one in which you are trained, such as typing or shorthand, you can practice. These tests are often very much like those given in business school or high school courses. For many of the other skills and aptitudes, however, no short-time preparation can be made. Skills and abilities natural to you or that you have developed throughout your lifetime are being tested.

Many of the general questions just described provide all the data needed to answer the questions and ask you to use your reasoning ability to find the answers. Your best preparation for these tests, as well as for tests of facts and ideas, is to be at your physical and mental best. You, no doubt, have your own methods of getting into an exam-taking mood and keeping "in shape." The next section lists some ideas on this subject.

IV. KINDS OF QUESTIONS

Only rarely is the "essay" question, which you answer in narrative form, used in civil service tests. Civil service tests are usually of the short-answer type. Full instructions for answering these questions will be given to you at the examination. But in case this is your first experience with short-answer questions and separate answer sheets, here is what you need to know:

1) Multiple-choice Questions

Most popular of the short-answer questions is the "multiple choice" or "best answer" question. It can be used, for example, to test for factual knowledge, ability to solve problems or judgment in meeting situations found at work.

A multiple-choice question is normally one of three types—
- It can begin with an incomplete statement followed by several possible endings. You are to find the one ending which *best* completes the statement, although some of the others may not be entirely wrong.
- It can also be a complete statement in the form of a question which is answered by choosing one of the statements listed.

- It can be in the form of a problem – again you select the best answer.

Here is an example of a multiple-choice question with a discussion which should give you some clues as to the method for choosing the right answer:

When an employee has a complaint about his assignment, the action which will *best* help him overcome his difficulty is to
   A. discuss his difficulty with his coworkers
   B. take the problem to the head of the organization
   C. take the problem to the person who gave him the assignment
   D. say nothing to anyone about his complaint

In answering this question, you should study each of the choices to find which is best. Consider choice "A" – Certainly an employee may discuss his complaint with fellow employees, but no change or improvement can result, and the complaint remains unresolved. Choice "B" is a poor choice since the head of the organization probably does not know what assignment you have been given, and taking your problem to him is known as "going over the head" of the supervisor. The supervisor, or person who made the assignment, is the person who can clarify it or correct any injustice. Choice "C" is, therefore, correct. To say nothing, as in choice "D," is unwise. Supervisors have and interest in knowing the problems employees are facing, and the employee is seeking a solution to his problem.

2) True/False Questions

The "true/false" or "right/wrong" form of question is sometimes used. Here a complete statement is given. Your job is to decide whether the statement is right or wrong.

SAMPLE: A roaming cell-phone call to a nearby city costs less than a non-roaming call to a distant city.

This statement is wrong, or false, since roaming calls are more expensive.

This is not a complete list of all possible question forms, although most of the others are variations of these common types. You will always get complete directions for answering questions. Be sure you understand *how* to mark your answers – ask questions until you do.

V. RECORDING YOUR ANSWERS

Computer terminals are used more and more today for many different kinds of exams.

For an examination with very few applicants, you may be told to record your answers in the test booklet itself. Separate answer sheets are much more common. If this separate answer sheet is to be scored by machine – and this is often the case – it is highly important that you mark your answers correctly in order to get credit.

An electronic scoring machine is often used in civil service offices because of the speed with which papers can be scored. Machine-scored answer sheets must be marked with a pencil, which will be given to you. This pencil has a high graphite content which responds to the electronic scoring machine. As a matter of fact, stray dots may register as answers, so do not let your pencil rest on the answer sheet while you are pondering the correct answer. Also, if your pencil lead breaks or is otherwise defective, ask for another.

Since the answer sheet will be dropped in a slot in the scoring machine, be careful not to bend the corners or get the paper crumpled.

The answer sheet normally has five vertical columns of numbers, with 30 numbers to a column. These numbers correspond to the question numbers in your test booklet. After each number, going across the page are four or five pairs of dotted lines. These short dotted lines have small letters or numbers above them. The first two pairs may also have a "T" or "F" above the letters. This indicates that the first two pairs only are to be used if the questions are of the true-false type. If the questions are multiple choice, disregard the "T" and "F" and pay attention only to the small letters or numbers.

Answer your questions in the manner of the sample that follows:

32. The largest city in the United States is
    A. Washington, D.C.
    B. New York City
    C. Chicago
    D. Detroit
    E. San Francisco

1) Choose the answer you think is best. (New York City is the largest, so "B" is correct.)
2) Find the row of dotted lines numbered the same as the question you are answering. (Find row number 32)
3) Find the pair of dotted lines corresponding to the answer. (Find the pair of lines under the mark "B.")
4) Make a solid black mark between the dotted lines.

VI. BEFORE THE TEST

Common sense will help you find procedures to follow to get ready for an examination. Too many of us, however, overlook these sensible measures. Indeed, nervousness and fatigue have been found to be the most serious reasons why applicants fail to do their best on civil service tests. Here is a list of reminders:

- Begin your preparation early – Don't wait until the last minute to go scurrying around for books and materials or to find out what the position is all about.
- Prepare continuously – An hour a night for a week is better than an all-night cram session. This has been definitely established. What is more, a night a week for a month will return better dividends than crowding your study into a shorter period of time.
- Locate the place of the exam – You have been sent a notice telling you when and where to report for the examination. If the location is in a different town or otherwise unfamiliar to you, it would be well to inquire the best route and learn something about the building.
- Relax the night before the test – Allow your mind to rest. Do not study at all that night. Plan some mild recreation or diversion; then go to bed early and get a good night's sleep.
- Get up early enough to make a leisurely trip to the place for the test – This way unforeseen events, traffic snarls, unfamiliar buildings, etc. will not upset you.
- Dress comfortably – A written test is not a fashion show. You will be known by number and not by name, so wear something comfortable.

- Leave excess paraphernalia at home – Shopping bags and odd bundles will get in your way. You need bring only the items mentioned in the official notice you received; usually everything you need is provided. Do not bring reference books to the exam. They will only confuse those last minutes and be taken away from you when in the test room.
- Arrive somewhat ahead of time – If because of transportation schedules you must get there very early, bring a newspaper or magazine to take your mind off yourself while waiting.
- Locate the examination room – When you have found the proper room, you will be directed to the seat or part of the room where you will sit. Sometimes you are given a sheet of instructions to read while you are waiting. Do not fill out any forms until you are told to do so; just read them and be prepared.
- Relax and prepare to listen to the instructions
- If you have any physical problem that may keep you from doing your best, be sure to tell the test administrator. If you are sick or in poor health, you really cannot do your best on the exam. You can come back and take the test some other time.

VII. AT THE TEST

The day of the test is here and you have the test booklet in your hand. The temptation to get going is very strong. Caution! There is more to success than knowing the right answers. You must know how to identify your papers and understand variations in the type of short-answer question used in this particular examination. Follow these suggestions for maximum results from your efforts:

1) Cooperate with the monitor

The test administrator has a duty to create a situation in which you can be as much at ease as possible. He will give instructions, tell you when to begin, check to see that you are marking your answer sheet correctly, and so on. He is not there to guard you, although he will see that your competitors do not take unfair advantage. He wants to help you do your best.

2) Listen to all instructions

Don't jump the gun! Wait until you understand all directions. In most civil service tests you get more time than you need to answer the questions. So don't be in a hurry. Read each word of instructions until you clearly understand the meaning. Study the examples, listen to all announcements and follow directions. Ask questions if you do not understand what to do.

3) Identify your papers

Civil service exams are usually identified by number only. You will be assigned a number; you must not put your name on your test papers. Be sure to copy your number correctly. Since more than one exam may be given, copy your exact examination title.

4) Plan your time

Unless you are told that a test is a "speed" or "rate of work" test, speed itself is usually not important. Time enough to answer all the questions will be provided, but this does not mean that you have all day. An overall time limit has been set. Divide the total time (in minutes) by the number of questions to determine the approximate time you have for each question.

5) Do not linger over difficult questions

If you come across a difficult question, mark it with a paper clip (useful to have along) and come back to it when you have been through the booklet. One caution if you do this – be sure to skip a number on your answer sheet as well. Check often to be sure that you have not lost your place and that you are marking in the row numbered the same as the question you are answering.

6) Read the questions

Be sure you know what the question asks! Many capable people are unsuccessful because they failed to *read* the questions correctly.

7) Answer all questions

Unless you have been instructed that a penalty will be deducted for incorrect answers, it is better to guess than to omit a question.

8) Speed tests

It is often better NOT to guess on speed tests. It has been found that on timed tests people are tempted to spend the last few seconds before time is called in marking answers at random – without even reading them – in the hope of picking up a few extra points. To discourage this practice, the instructions may warn you that your score will be "corrected" for guessing. That is, a penalty will be applied. The incorrect answers will be deducted from the correct ones, or some other penalty formula will be used.

9) Review your answers

If you finish before time is called, go back to the questions you guessed or omitted to give them further thought. Review other answers if you have time.

10) Return your test materials

If you are ready to leave before others have finished or time is called, take ALL your materials to the monitor and leave quietly. Never take any test material with you. The monitor can discover whose papers are not complete, and taking a test booklet may be grounds for disqualification.

VIII. EXAMINATION TECHNIQUES

1) Read the general instructions carefully. These are usually printed on the first page of the exam booklet. As a rule, these instructions refer to the timing of the examination; the fact that you should not start work until the signal and must stop work at a signal, etc. If there are any *special* instructions, such as a choice of questions to be answered, make sure that you note this instruction carefully.

2) When you are ready to start work on the examination, that is as soon as the signal has been given, read the instructions to each question booklet, underline any key words or phrases, such as *least*, *best*, *outline*, *describe* and the like. In this way you will tend to answer as requested rather than discover on reviewing your paper that you *listed without describing*, that you selected the *worst* choice rather than the *best* choice, etc.

3) If the examination is of the objective or multiple-choice type – that is, each question will also give a series of possible answers: A, B, C or D, and you are called upon to select the best answer and write the letter next to that answer on your answer paper – it is advisable to start answering each question in turn. There may be anywhere from 50 to 100 such questions in the three or four hours allotted and you can see how much time would be taken if you read through all the questions before beginning to answer any. Furthermore, if you come across a question or group of questions which you know would be difficult to answer, it would undoubtedly affect your handling of all the other questions.

4) If the examination is of the essay type and contains but a few questions, it is a moot point as to whether you should read all the questions before starting to answer any one. Of course, if you are given a choice – say five out of seven and the like – then it is essential to read all the questions so you can eliminate the two that are most difficult. If, however, you are asked to answer all the questions, there may be danger in trying to answer the easiest one first because you may find that you will spend too much time on it. The best technique is to answer the first question, then proceed to the second, etc.

5) Time your answers. Before the exam begins, write down the time it started, then add the time allowed for the examination and write down the time it must be completed, then divide the time available somewhat as follows:
    - If 3-1/2 hours are allowed, that would be 210 minutes. If you have 80 objective-type questions, that would be an average of 2-1/2 minutes per question. Allow yourself no more than 2 minutes per question, or a total of 160 minutes, which will permit about 50 minutes to review.
    - If for the time allotment of 210 minutes there are 7 essay questions to answer, that would average about 30 minutes a question. Give yourself only 25 minutes per question so that you have about 35 minutes to review.

6) The most important instruction is to *read each question* and make sure you know what is wanted. The second most important instruction is to *time yourself properly* so that you answer every question. The third most important instruction is to *answer every question*. Guess if you have to but include something for each question. Remember that you will receive no credit for a blank and will probably receive some credit if you write something in answer to an essay question. If you guess a letter – say "B" for a multiple-choice question – you may have guessed right. If you leave a blank as an answer to a multiple-choice question, the examiners may respect your feelings but it will not add a point to your score. Some exams may penalize you for wrong answers, so in such cases *only*, you may not want to guess unless you have some basis for your answer.

7) Suggestions
    a. Objective-type questions
        1. Examine the question booklet for proper sequence of pages and questions
        2. Read all instructions carefully
        3. Skip any question which seems too difficult; return to it after all other questions have been answered
        4. Apportion your time properly; do not spend too much time on any single question or group of questions

5. Note and underline key words – *all, most, fewest, least, best, worst, same, opposite*, etc.
6. Pay particular attention to negatives
7. Note unusual option, e.g., unduly long, short, complex, different or similar in content to the body of the question
8. Observe the use of "hedging" words – *probably, may, most likely*, etc.
9. Make sure that your answer is put next to the same number as the question
10. Do not second-guess unless you have good reason to believe the second answer is definitely more correct
11. Cross out original answer if you decide another answer is more accurate; do not erase until you are ready to hand your paper in
12. Answer all questions; guess unless instructed otherwise
13. Leave time for review

b. Essay questions
1. Read each question carefully
2. Determine exactly what is wanted. Underline key words or phrases.
3. Decide on outline or paragraph answer
4. Include many different points and elements unless asked to develop any one or two points or elements
5. Show impartiality by giving pros and cons unless directed to select one side only
6. Make and write down any assumptions you find necessary to answer the questions
7. Watch your English, grammar, punctuation and choice of words
8. Time your answers; don't crowd material

8) Answering the essay question

Most essay questions can be answered by framing the specific response around several key words or ideas. Here are a few such key words or ideas:

M's: manpower, materials, methods, money, management
P's: purpose, program, policy, plan, procedure, practice, problems, pitfalls, personnel, public relations

a. Six basic steps in handling problems:
1. Preliminary plan and background development
2. Collect information, data and facts
3. Analyze and interpret information, data and facts
4. Analyze and develop solutions as well as make recommendations
5. Prepare report and sell recommendations
6. Install recommendations and follow up effectiveness

b. Pitfalls to avoid
1. *Taking things for granted* – A statement of the situation does not necessarily imply that each of the elements is necessarily true; for example, a complaint may be invalid and biased so that all that can be taken for granted is that a complaint has been registered

2. *Considering only one side of a situation* – Wherever possible, indicate several alternatives and then point out the reasons you selected the best one
3. *Failing to indicate follow up* – Whenever your answer indicates action on your part, make certain that you will take proper follow-up action to see how successful your recommendations, procedures or actions turn out to be
4. *Taking too long in answering any single question* – Remember to time your answers properly

IX. AFTER THE TEST

Scoring procedures differ in detail among civil service jurisdictions although the general principles are the same. Whether the papers are hand-scored or graded by machine we have described, they are nearly always graded by number. That is, the person who marks the paper knows only the number – never the name – of the applicant. Not until all the papers have been graded will they be matched with names. If other tests, such as training and experience or oral interview ratings have been given, scores will be combined. Different parts of the examination usually have different weights. For example, the written test might count 60 percent of the final grade, and a rating of training and experience 40 percent. In many jurisdictions, veterans will have a certain number of points added to their grades.

After the final grade has been determined, the names are placed in grade order and an eligible list is established. There are various methods for resolving ties between those who get the same final grade – probably the most common is to place first the name of the person whose application was received first. Job offers are made from the eligible list in the order the names appear on it. You will be notified of your grade and your rank as soon as all these computations have been made. This will be done as rapidly as possible.

People who are found to meet the requirements in the announcement are called "eligibles." Their names are put on a list of eligible candidates. An eligible's chances of getting a job depend on how high he stands on this list and how fast agencies are filling jobs from the list.

When a job is to be filled from a list of eligibles, the agency asks for the names of people on the list of eligibles for that job. When the civil service commission receives this request, it sends to the agency the names of the three people highest on this list. Or, if the job to be filled has specialized requirements, the office sends the agency the names of the top three persons who meet these requirements from the general list.

The appointing officer makes a choice from among the three people whose names were sent to him. If the selected person accepts the appointment, the names of the others are put back on the list to be considered for future openings.

That is the rule in hiring from all kinds of eligible lists, whether they are for typist, carpenter, chemist, or something else. For every vacancy, the appointing officer has his choice of any one of the top three eligibles on the list. This explains why the person whose name is on top of the list sometimes does not get an appointment when some of the persons lower on the list do. If the appointing officer chooses the second or third eligible, the No. 1 eligible does not get a job at once, but stays on the list until he is appointed or the list is terminated.

X. HOW TO PASS THE INTERVIEW TEST

The examination for which you applied requires an oral interview test. You have already taken the written test and you are now being called for the interview test – the final part of the formal examination.

You may think that it is not possible to prepare for an interview test and that there are no procedures to follow during an interview. Our purpose is to point out some things you can do in advance that will help you and some good rules to follow and pitfalls to avoid while you are being interviewed.

What is an interview supposed to test?

The written examination is designed to test the technical knowledge and competence of the candidate; the oral is designed to evaluate intangible qualities, not readily measured otherwise, and to establish a list showing the relative fitness of each candidate – as measured against his competitors – for the position sought. Scoring is not on the basis of "right" and "wrong," but on a sliding scale of values ranging from "not passable" to "outstanding." As a matter of fact, it is possible to achieve a relatively low score without a single "incorrect" answer because of evident weakness in the qualities being measured.

Occasionally, an examination may consist entirely of an oral test – either an individual or a group oral. In such cases, information is sought concerning the technical knowledges and abilities of the candidate, since there has been no written examination for this purpose. More commonly, however, an oral test is used to supplement a written examination.

Who conducts interviews?

The composition of oral boards varies among different jurisdictions. In nearly all, a representative of the personnel department serves as chairman. One of the members of the board may be a representative of the department in which the candidate would work. In some cases, "outside experts" are used, and, frequently, a businessman or some other representative of the general public is asked to serve. Labor and management or other special groups may be represented. The aim is to secure the services of experts in the appropriate field.

However the board is composed, it is a good idea (and not at all improper or unethical) to ascertain in advance of the interview who the members are and what groups they represent. When you are introduced to them, you will have some idea of their backgrounds and interests, and at least you will not stutter and stammer over their names.

What should be done before the interview?

While knowledge about the board members is useful and takes some of the surprise element out of the interview, there is other preparation which is more substantive. It *is* possible to prepare for an oral interview – in several ways:

1) Keep a copy of your application and review it carefully before the interview

This may be the only document before the oral board, and the starting point of the interview. Know what education and experience you have listed there, and the sequence and dates of all of it. Sometimes the board will ask you to review the highlights of your experience for them; you should not have to hem and haw doing it.

2) Study the class specification and the examination announcement

Usually, the oral board has one or both of these to guide them. The qualities, characteristics or knowledges required by the position sought are stated in these documents. They offer valuable clues as to the nature of the oral interview. For example, if the job involves supervisory responsibilities, the announcement will usually indicate that knowledge of modern supervisory methods and the qualifications of the candidate as a supervisor will be tested. If so, you can expect such questions, frequently in the form of a hypothetical situation which you are expected to solve. NEVER go into an oral without knowledge of the duties and responsibilities of the job you seek.

3) Think through each qualification required

Try to visualize the kind of questions you would ask if you were a board member. How well could you answer them? Try especially to appraise your own knowledge and background in each area, *measured against the job sought*, and identify any areas in which you are weak. Be critical and realistic – do not flatter yourself.

4) Do some general reading in areas in which you feel you may be weak

For example, if the job involves supervision and your past experience has NOT, some general reading in supervisory methods and practices, particularly in the field of human relations, might be useful. Do NOT study agency procedures or detailed manuals. The oral board will be testing your understanding and capacity, not your memory.

5) Get a good night's sleep and watch your general health and mental attitude

You will want a clear head at the interview. Take care of a cold or any other minor ailment, and of course, no hangovers.

What should be done on the day of the interview?

Now comes the day of the interview itself. Give yourself plenty of time to get there. Plan to arrive somewhat ahead of the scheduled time, particularly if your appointment is in the fore part of the day. If a previous candidate fails to appear, the board might be ready for you a bit early. By early afternoon an oral board is almost invariably behind schedule if there are many candidates, and you may have to wait. Take along a book or magazine to read, or your application to review, but leave any extraneous material in the waiting room when you go in for your interview. In any event, relax and compose yourself.

The matter of dress is important. The board is forming impressions about you – from your experience, your manners, your attitude, and your appearance. Give your personal appearance careful attention. Dress your best, but not your flashiest. Choose conservative, appropriate clothing, and be sure it is immaculate. This is a business interview, and your appearance should indicate that you regard it as such. Besides, being well groomed and properly dressed will help boost your confidence.

Sooner or later, someone will call your name and escort you into the interview room. *This is it.* From here on you are on your own. It is too late for any more preparation. But remember, you asked for this opportunity to prove your fitness, and you are here because your request was granted.

What happens when you go in?

The usual sequence of events will be as follows: The clerk (who is often the board stenographer) will introduce you to the chairman of the oral board, who will introduce you to the other members of the board. Acknowledge the introductions before you sit down. Do not be surprised if you find a microphone facing you or a stenotypist sitting by. Oral interviews are usually recorded in the event of an appeal or other review.

Usually the chairman of the board will open the interview by reviewing the highlights of your education and work experience from your application – primarily for the benefit of the other members of the board, as well as to get the material into the record. Do not interrupt or comment unless there is an error or significant misinterpretation; if that is the case, do not hesitate. But do not quibble about insignificant matters. Also, he will usually ask you some question about your education, experience or your present job – partly to get you to start talking and to establish the interviewing "rapport." He may start the actual questioning, or turn it over to one of the other members. Frequently, each member undertakes the questioning on a particular area, one in which he is perhaps most competent, so you can expect each member to participate in the examination. Because time is limited, you may also expect some rather abrupt switches in the direction the questioning takes, so do not be upset by it. Normally, a board member will not pursue a single line of questioning unless he discovers a particular strength or weakness.

After each member has participated, the chairman will usually ask whether any member has any further questions, then will ask you if you have anything you wish to add. Unless you are expecting this question, it may floor you. Worse, it may start you off on an extended, extemporaneous speech. The board is not usually seeking more information. The question is principally to offer you a last opportunity to present further qualifications or to indicate that you have nothing to add. So, if you feel that a significant qualification or characteristic has been overlooked, it is proper to point it out in a sentence or so. Do not compliment the board on the thoroughness of their examination -- they have been sketchy, and you know it. If you wish, merely say, "No thank you, I have nothing further to add." This is a point where you can "talk yourself out" of a good impression or fail to present an important bit of information. Remember, *you close the interview yourself*.

The chairman will then say, "That is all, Mr. _____, thank you." Do not be startled; the interview is over, and quicker than you think. Thank him, gather your belongings and take your leave. Save your sigh of relief for the other side of the door.

How to put your best foot forward

Throughout this entire process, you may feel that the board individually and collectively is trying to pierce your defenses, seek out your hidden weaknesses and embarrass and confuse you. Actually, this is not true. They are obliged to make an appraisal of your qualifications for the job you are seeking, and they want to see you in your best light. Remember, they must interview all candidates and a non-cooperative candidate may become a failure in spite of their best efforts to bring out his qualifications. Here are 15 suggestions that will help you:

1) Be natural – Keep your attitude confident, not cocky

If you are not confident that you can do the job, do not expect the board to be. Do not apologize for your weaknesses, try to bring out your strong points. The board is interested in a positive, not negative, presentation. Cockiness will antagonize any board member and make him wonder if you are covering up a weakness by a false show of strength.

2) Get comfortable, but don't lounge or sprawl

Sit erectly but not stiffly. A careless posture may lead the board to conclude that you are careless in other things, or at least that you are not impressed by the importance of the occasion. Either conclusion is natural, even if incorrect. Do not fuss with your clothing, a pencil or an ashtray. Your hands may occasionally be useful to emphasize a point; do not let them become a point of distraction.

3) Do not wisecrack or make small talk

This is a serious situation, and your attitude should show that you consider it as such. Further, the time of the board is limited – they do not want to waste it, and neither should you.

4) Do not exaggerate your experience or abilities

In the first place, from information in the application or other interviews and sources, the board may know more about you than you think. Secondly, you probably will not get away with it. An experienced board is rather adept at spotting such a situation, so do not take the chance.

5) If you know a board member, do not make a point of it, yet do not hide it

Certainly you are not fooling him, and probably not the other members of the board. Do not try to take advantage of your acquaintanceship – it will probably do you little good.

6) Do not dominate the interview

Let the board do that. They will give you the clues – do not assume that you have to do all the talking. Realize that the board has a number of questions to ask you, and do not try to take up all the interview time by showing off your extensive knowledge of the answer to the first one.

7) Be attentive

You only have 20 minutes or so, and you should keep your attention at its sharpest throughout. When a member is addressing a problem or question to you, give him your undivided attention. Address your reply principally to him, but do not exclude the other board members.

8) Do not interrupt

A board member may be stating a problem for you to analyze. He will ask you a question when the time comes. Let him state the problem, and wait for the question.

9) Make sure you understand the question

Do not try to answer until you are sure what the question is. If it is not clear, restate it in your own words or ask the board member to clarify it for you. However, do not haggle about minor elements.

10) Reply promptly but not hastily

A common entry on oral board rating sheets is "candidate responded readily," or "candidate hesitated in replies." Respond as promptly and quickly as you can, but do not jump to a hasty, ill-considered answer.

11) Do not be peremptory in your answers

A brief answer is proper – but do not fire your answer back. That is a losing game from your point of view. The board member can probably ask questions much faster than you can answer them.

12) Do not try to create the answer you think the board member wants

He is interested in what kind of mind you have and how it works – not in playing games. Furthermore, he can usually spot this practice and will actually grade you down on it.

13) Do not switch sides in your reply merely to agree with a board member

Frequently, a member will take a contrary position merely to draw you out and to see if you are willing and able to defend your point of view. Do not start a debate, yet do not surrender a good position. If a position is worth taking, it is worth defending.

14) Do not be afraid to admit an error in judgment if you are shown to be wrong

The board knows that you are forced to reply without any opportunity for careful consideration. Your answer may be demonstrably wrong. If so, admit it and get on with the interview.

15) Do not dwell at length on your present job

The opening question may relate to your present assignment. Answer the question but do not go into an extended discussion. You are being examined for a *new* job, not your present one. As a matter of fact, try to phrase ALL your answers in terms of the job for which you are being examined.

Basis of Rating

Probably you will forget most of these "do's" and "don'ts" when you walk into the oral interview room. Even remembering them all will not ensure you a passing grade. Perhaps you did not have the qualifications in the first place. But remembering them will help you to put your best foot forward, without treading on the toes of the board members.

Rumor and popular opinion to the contrary notwithstanding, an oral board wants you to make the best appearance possible. They know you are under pressure – but they also want to see how you respond to it as a guide to what your reaction would be under the pressures of the job you seek. They will be influenced by the degree of poise you display, the personal traits you show and the manner in which you respond.

ABOUT THIS BOOK

This book contains tests divided into Examination Sections. Go through each test, answering every question in the margin. We have also attached a sample answer sheet at the back of the book that can be removed and used. At the end of each test look at the answer key and check your answers. On the ones you got wrong, look at the right answer choice and learn. Do not fill in the answers first. Do not memorize the questions and answers, but understand the answer and principles involved. On your test, the questions will likely be different from the samples. Questions are changed and new ones added. If you understand these past questions you should have success with any changes that arise. Tests may consist of several types of questions. We have additional books on each subject should more study be advisable or necessary for you. Finally, the more you study, the better prepared you will be. This book is intended to be the last thing you study before you walk into the examination room. Prior study of relevant texts is also recommended. NLC publishes some of these in our Fundamental Series. Knowledge and good sense are important factors in passing your exam. Good luck also helps. So now study this Passbook, absorb the material contained within and take that knowledge into the examination. Then do your best to pass that exam.

EXAMINATION SECTION

EXAMINATION SECTION
TEST 1

DIRECTIONS: Each question or incomplete statement is followed by several suggested answers or completions. Select the one that BEST answers the question or completes the statement. *PRINT THE LETTER OF THE CORRECT ANSWER IN THE SPACE AT THE RIGHT.*

Questions 1-5.

DIRECTIONS: Arrange the following names in alphabetical order as they would appear on the hold shelf of a library by matching the name in Column A with its order position in Column B.

	Column A		Column B	
1.	Smiles, Roy	A.	First	1.____
		B.	Second	
2.	Smigel, Robert	C.	Third	2.____
		D.	Fourth	
3.	Smith, Raymond	E.	Fifth	3.____
4.	Smith, Rhonda			4.____
5.	Smiegel, Rayna			5.____

Questions 6-10.

DIRECTIONS: Each of Questions 6 through 10 may be:
    A. Incorrect due to improper spelling
    B. Incorrect due to improper punctuation
    C. Incorrect due to improper capitalization
    D. Correct

6. The reference section is non-circulating, this means you can't check these items out.   6.____

7. The book can be found in the non-ficton section of the library.   7.____

8. Biographies are a popular selection among all age groups at our library.   8.____

9. The elm grove library is the third biggest library in the county.   9.____

10. Since your book was one week overdue, I cannot wave this fine for you.   10.____

Questions 11-15.

DIRECTIONS: Questions 11 through 15 are to be answered SOLELY on the basis of the information given in the following paragraph.

    Libraries have a long history, with the oldest recorded library dating back to Ancient Egypt circa 367 BC to 283 BC. In recent years, however, technological developments have changed the nature of library service. The rise of the internet and the growing number of digital libraries have resulted in a decrease in library usage. Throughout history, library service has primarily focused on the collection of books and other resources a library offers to its patrons. This collection-centered approach to library service has been challenged by the public's ability to access much of this information virtually without ever stepping inside of a library. Fortunately, there is another approach to library service that remains useful and relevant in the digital age: a user-centered approach. A user-centered approach shifts the focus from a library's physical collection to the services it provides to promote learning and social interaction among its users.

11. Based on what you've read in the above paragraph, which of the following would be an example of user-centered library service?
    A. A library's acquisition of a rare manuscript
    B. The expansion of a library's digital collection
    C. The installation of more shelving to house a larger and more diverse collection
    D. the creation of a librarian-led study group for adult learners returning to school

12. According to the above paragraph, libraries have been around for about _____ years.
    A. 500   B. 2,300   C. 1,700   D. 100

13. According to the above paragraph, what has made a collection-centered approach to library service less useful?
    A. Poor collection development   B. A decrease in book prices
    C. Technological advancements   D. A more educated public

14. Based on what you've read in the above paragraph, what must libraries do to remain relevant in the modern age?
    A. Adopt a user-centered approach to library service
    B. Adopt a collection-centered approach to library service
    C. Seek funding from new sources
    D. Abandon physical collections for completely digital collections

15. Based on what you've read in the above paragraph, which of the following BEST describes the difference between collection-centered and user-centered library service?
    Collection-centered library service focuses on _____, while user-centered library service focuses on _____.
    A. the services a library offers that promote learning and socialization; a library's physical holdings of books and resources
    B. digitizing a library's entire collection; maintaining a physical collection

C. maintaining a physical collection; digitizing a library's entire collection
D. a library's physical holdings of books and resources; the services a library offers that promote learning and socialization

Questions 16-20.

DIRECTIONS: Questions 16 through 20 each consist of four call numbers in Column A and Column B. Compare the numbers listed in each column and use the following to provide your answer:
A. One call number in Column A and Column B are the same
B. Two call numbers in Column A and Column B are the same
C. Three call numbers in Column A and Column B are the same
D. All four call numbers in Column A and Column B are the same

	Column A	Column B	
16.	696.45 BAC 645.96 CAB 656.46 DAN 646.56 AND	696.45 CAB 645.96 BAC 656.46 DAN 646.56 AND	16.____
17.	251.84 NEJ 258.14 ENE 284.84 NEE 248.15 JEE	251.84 NEJ 258.14 ENE 284.84 NEE 248.15 JEE	17.____
18.	199.33 WEN 139.93 WEW 113.31 NEW 133.99 WEE	199.33 WEN 139.93 WEN 113.31 WEW 133.93 WEE	18.____
19.	823.65 HOW 832.56 WHO 862.35 WOW 856.23 WON	823.65 HOW 823.56 WHO 862.35 WOW 856.23 WON	19.____
20.	429.55 BEB 495.22 BEE 422.95 EBB 492.59 EBE	429.55 BEB 492.22 BEE 422.95 EBB 495.29 EBE	20.____

Questions 21-25.

DIRECTIONS: Questions 21 through 25 are to be answered on the basis of the following table.

Dry Creek Library Monthly Adult Program Records				
Program	Number of Attendees Ages 18-24	Number of Attendees Ages 25-44	Number of Attendees Ages 45-65	Number of Attendees Age 65+
Writers' Group	4	5	4	3
Knitting Circle	4	3	3	2
Tai Chi	3	4	1	6
Mystery Book Club	0	2	3	4
Non-Fiction Book Club	2	5	4	3

21. Which program has the HIGHEST attendance rate? 21.____
    A. Writers' Group   B. Tai Chi
    C. Non-Fiction Book Club D. Knitting Circle

22. Which age group has the HIGHEST participation rate in monthly library programs? 22.____
    A. 18-24   B. 25-44   C. 45-65   D. 65+

23. Which program is MOST popular among 18 to 44 year olds? 23.____
    A. Writers' Group   B. Knitting Club
    C. Mystery Book Club   D. Non-Fiction Book Club

24. If the library were to discontinue a program, which program would be the MOST logical choice based upon these program records? 24.____
    A. Writers' Group   B. Tai Chi
    C. Mystery Book Club   D. Knitting Circle

25. If the library wants to expand one program from monthly to weekly in order to attract more seniors, which program would be the MOST logical choice based on these program records? 25.____
    A. Writers' Group   B. Knitting Circle
    C. Mystery Book Club   D. Tai Chi

KEY (CORRECT ANSWERS)

1.	C		11.	D
2.	B		12.	B
3.	D		13.	C
4.	E		14.	A
5.	A		15.	D
6.	B		16.	B
7.	A		17.	D
8.	D		18.	A
9.	C		19.	C
10.	A		20.	B

21. A
22. B
23. A
24. C
25. D

TEST 2

DIRECTIONS: Each question or incomplete statement is followed by several suggested answers or completions. Select the one that BEST answers the question or completes the statement. *PRINT THE LETTER OF THE CORRECT ANSWER IN THE SPACE AT THE RIGHT.*

1. Which of the following words is spelled INCORRECTLY? 1.____
   A. microfiche   B. photocopyer   C. interlibrary   D. catalog

2. Which of the following sentences includes an error in punctuation? 2.____
   A. I'm holding Mr. Rutgers book at the circulation desk.
   B. All meeting rooms are currently reserved.
   C. Only library cardholders can request books through interlibrary loan.
   D. Children's books are located upstairs in the Youth Services Department.

3. Which of the following sentences includes a capitalization error? 3.____
   A. The library director must sign off on all purchases.
   B. This week the Ashton Public Library Book Club is reading *The Paris Wife*.
   C. If you need help with academic research, you should speak with a librarian in the department of reference services.
   D. Our most popular program is our weekly Gourmet Club, where people come together to talk about fine food and drinks.

4. Which of the following words is spelled INCORRECTLY? 4.____
   A. biography   B. anthology   C. magizine   D. bibliography

5. Which of the following sentences includes an error in punctuation? 5.____
   A. Can I see your driver's license?
   B. Ms. Janda said that she would be arriving 10 minutes late for the computer class.
   C. There are only three copies left of the book selected for the monthly book club.
   D. Who did you speak to over the phone about this hold request.

Questions 6-10.

DIRECTIONS: Questions 6 through 10 include sentences with one word underlined. For each question, please select the word with the CLOSEST meaning to the underlined word.

6. Mr. Banks has a block on his account because he has too many <u>fines</u>. 6.____
   A. charges   B. items   C. warnings   D. restrictions

7. *The Girl With the Dragon Tattoo* received overwhelmingly positive <u>reviews</u>. 7.____
   A. investments   B. reassessments
   C. critiques   D. inspections

8. When you write a research paper, you must include <u>citations</u>. 8.____
   A. commendations B. references
   C. facts D. inferences

9. If you make a copy of that CD, you are <u>infringing</u> upon copyright law. 9.____
   A. preserving B. misunderstanding
   C. violating D. elucidating

10. *Architectural Digest* is located on the first floor with the other <u>serials</u>. 10.____
    A. books   B. databases   C. periodicals   D. archives

Questions 11-15.

DIRECTIONS: Questions 11 through 15 consist of four addresses in Column A and Column B. Compare the addresses listed in each column and use the following to provide your answer:
   A. One address in Column A and Column B are the same.
   B. Two addresses in Column A and Column B are the same.
   C. Three addresses in Column A and Column B are the same.
   D. All four addresses in Column A and Column B are the same.

<u>Column A</u>

<u>Column B</u>

11. 3941 Blackwell Dr.
    3491 Blackwell Dr.
    3991 Blackswell St.
    3945 Blackstreet Ave.

    3941 Blackwell Dr.
    3914 Balckwell Dr.
    3941 Blackwell St.
    3945 Blackstreet Dr.   11.____

12. 204 Rhodes Ave. Apt. B
    206 Rhodes Ave. Apt. 6
    206 Rhoades Ave. Apt B
    260 Rhodes St. Apt. B6

    204 Rhodes Ave. Apt. B
    204 Rhodes Ave. Apt 4
    206 Rhoades Ave. Apt. B
    260 Rhodes St. Apt. B6   12.____

13. 1155 Judith Rd.
    1515 Judith Ln.
    5111 Judy Rd.
    1155 Judy Ln.

    1155 Judith Rd.
    1515 Judith Ln.
    5111 Judy Rd.
    1155 Judy Ln.   13.____

14. 2367 Cascade Blvd.
    7632 Cascade Ave.
    2367 Cascadia Blvd.
    7632 Cascade Blvd.

    2376 Cascade Blvd.
    7632 Cascade Ave.
    2367 Cascadia Blvd.
    7632 Cascadia Blvd.   14.____

15. 106 Brooks Ln. Apt. 12
    102 Brooks Ln. Apt. 16
    126 Brook Ln. Apt. 11
    162 Brook Ave. Apt. 2

    106 Brooks Ln. Apt. 12
    102 Brooks Ln. Apt. 16
    126 Brooks Ln. Apt. 11
    166 Brook Ave. Apt. 2   15.____

Questions 16-20.

DIRECTIONS: In Questions 16 through 20, please match the author's last name in Column A with its proper order on the shelf of a library that organizes fiction alphabetically by author's last name in Column B.

Column A   Column B

16. Brockenstein   A. First   16.____
                        B. Second
17. Brock   C. Third   17.____
                        D. Fourth
18. Broadchurch   E. Fifth   18.____

19. Broadbent   19.____

20. Brockley   20.____

21. If a patron returns five books two days past their due date, and overdue   21.____
    charges accrue at 15 cents per day for each book, how much does the patron
    owe in overdue fees?
    A. $1.50   B. $0.75   C. $3.00   D. $5.75

22. Susan is compiling statistics from monthly library usage records. Records   22.____
    state that over the course of one month, patrons checked out 5,375 adult fiction
    titles, 4,789 adult non-fiction titles, 6,854 audio-visual items, and 3,632
    magazines. Based on these records, fiction titles comprise about _____
    percent of overall monthly circulation.
    A. 52   B. 26   C. 15   D. 38

23. Yearly statistics show that over the course of one week an average of 33   23.____
    patrons attend library programs. If there are four programs scheduled during
    one week, about how many patrons will be attending each program?
    A. 3   B. 11   C. 5   D. 8

24. Jane is calling patrons to inform them that the interlibrary loan books they 24.____
    requested have arrived. It takes Jane approximately five minutes to notify each
    patron, and she has a cart filled with 37 interlibrary books that require patron
    notification. She also has a bin full of returned books that need to be checked
    in and shelved. How long will it take Jane to finish the hold notifications so she
    can move on to her next task?
    A. One hour   B. About six hours
    C. About three hours   D. 45 minutes

25. Birch Grove Library has a rule that patrons can only check out 50 books at a time, 50 audio-visual items at a time, and 15 interlibrary loan items at a time. The library also has a rule that no more than 75 items total can be checked out to a patron's account at one time. If a patron already has 45 books, 25 audio-visual items, and 5 interlibrary loan items checked out, she can

    A. still check out 5 books, 25 audio-visual items, 5 interlibrary loan items
    B. no longer check anything out until she returns some of her items
    C. still check out 30 books
    D. still check out 10 interlibrary loan items and 25 audio-visual items

25.____

KEY (CORRECT ANSWERS)

1.	B		11.	A
2.	A		12.	C
3.	C		13.	D
4.	C		14.	B
5.	D		15.	B
6.	A		16.	D
7.	C		17.	C
8.	B		18.	B
9.	C		19.	A
10.	C		20.	E

21. A
22. B
23. D
24. C
25. B

TEST 3

DIRECTIONS: Each question or incomplete statement is followed by several suggested answers or completions. Select the one that BEST answers the question or completes the statement. *PRINT THE LETTER OF THE CORRECT ANSWER IN THE SPACE AT THE RIGHT.*

Questions 1-5.

DIRECTIONS: Questions 1 through 5 are to be answered on the basis of the following paragraph.

    Copyright law plays an important role in how libraries operate and provide information to their patrons. Libraries must abide by state and federal copyright laws, including the Copyright Act, which is the most authoritative source of copyright law in the United States. Through the Copyright Act's first sale doctrine, libraries are allowed to lend books and other copyrighted material. Additionally, the Copyright Act's fair use law allows library patrons to use copyrighted materials for specific functions, such as criticism, comment, news reporting, scholarship, and research. Copyright law also allows libraries to reproduce copyrighted works in order to preserve or replace these works or provide them to people with disabilities.

1. Which of the following would NOT be an acceptable reason for a library to reproduce copyrighted material?
   A. To deliver it to a person who is housebound due to a physical disability
   B. To sell it in the library's book sale in order to raise funds for the library's remodel
   C. To preserve a book that is currently out of print and that also has limited used copies available
   D. To replace a copy of a rare book that has been lost

1.____

2. Which law allows libraries to lend books and other copyrighted materials?
   A. This is not allowed under state or federal law
   B. The fair use law
   C. The first sale doctrine
   D. The first use act

2.____

3. Based on the fair use law, libraries can allow patrons to quote or use passages from copyrighted materials in
   A. newspaper articles
   B. business brochures
   C. book manuscripts set for publication
   D. television advertisements

3.____

4. In the United States, copyright law PRIMARILY comes from
   A. state law   B. the first use act
   C. municipal law   D. the Copyright Act

4.____

5. The fair use law can be found in
   A. state law
   B. the Copyright Act
   C. the First Amendment
   D. municipal law

6. Which of the following words is spelled INCORRECTLY?
   A. alamnac
   B. dictionary
   C. atlas
   D. encyclopedia

7. Which of the following sentences contains an error in punctuation?
   A. There are two titles on hold for members of the library's book club: *Gone Girl* and *Me Before You*.
   B. At the beginning of each month the library director holds a staff meeting that everyone is required to attend.
   C. Did you ask the patron for her photo I.D. before providing her with her account information?
   D. The library's Knitting Circle meets the first Thursday, second Saturday and third Monday of every month.

8. Which of the following words is spelled INCORRECTLY?
   A. classification
   B. plagarism
   C. withdrawn
   D. volume

9. Which of the following sentences includes an error in capitalization?
   A. All of the items you had on hold were sent back Tuesday.
   B. Did Mr. Phekos register for this week's cooking demonstration?
   C. Tanner is helping with the fundraiser because he is a member of the friends of the library.
   D. Book donations can be placed in the donation box near the circulation desk.

10. Which of the following words is spelled INCORRECTLY?
    A. thesarus
    B. thesis
    C. series
    D. reserve

Questions 11-15.

DIRECTIONS: Questions 11 through 15 each contain three lines of letters in Column A and three lines of numbers in Column B. The letters in each line should correspond with the numbers in each line as outlined in the following table:

Letter	J	R	D	T	M	C	P	K	O	S
Matching Number	0	1	2	3	4	5	6	7	8	9

Please answer the questions as follows:
A. None of the lines of letters and lines of numbers are matched correctly.
B. One of the lines of letters and numbers is matched correctly.
C. Two of the lines of letters and lines of numbers are matched correctly.
D. All three of the lines of letters and lines of numbers are matched correctly.

Column A	Column B	
11. JMCP RMKS CPRO	0456 1479 5618	11.____
12. DRKS MKPJ JDCP	9172 4761 0256	12.____
13. CSDJ RKRD JKPC	5924 1712 0765	13.____
14. TMMO CPDR JOTS	3448 5632 0839	14.____
15. JCMS ROST MKJD	0648 1983 4701	15.____

Questions 16-20.

DIRECTIONS: In Questions 16 through 20, match the book title in Column A with its proper alphabetical orders based on letter by letter filing rules.

Column A	Column B	
16. To Kill a Mockingbird	A. First	16.____
17. A Tale of Two Cities	B. Second C. Third	17.____
18. The Time Traveler's Wife	D. Fourth E. Fifth	18.____
19. Treasure Island		19.____
20. The Two Towers		20.____

Questions 21-25.

DIRECTIONS: Questions 21 through 25 are to be answered on the basis of the following table.

Dry Creek Library 2023 Library Card Registration by Season					
Season	Number of Registrants Under 18	Number of Registrants Ages 18-24	Number of Registrants Ages 25-44	Number of Registrants Ages 45-65	Number of Registrants Age 65+
Winter	56	34	69	48	34
Spring	72	47	55	62	48
Summer	100	75	71	89	101
Fall	96	115	88	72	63

21. During which season does Dry Creek Library experience the MOST library card registrations?
    A. Winter B. Spring C. Summer D. Fall

22. Which of the following age groups registered for the MOST library cards in 2023?
    A. Under 18 B. 18-24 C. 25-44 D. 45-65

23. Which of the following patrons is MOST likely to register for a library card in the fall based on the data shown in the above table?
    A. A 10-year-old preparing for the new school year
    B. A 65-year-old who has just retired from his full-time job
    C. An 18-year-old entering her first semester of college
    D. A 26-year-old enrolled in medical school

24. During which season should Dry Creek Library increase marketing efforts to draw in more registrants between the ages of 18 and 24?
    A. Winter B. Spring C. Summer D. Fall

25. In 2022, 1,364 people registered for new library cards. How does this number compare to the number of registrants in 2023?
    It is _____ registered in 2023.
    A. the same amount of people that
    B. slightly less than the number of people who
    C. significantly more than the number of people who
    D. significantly less than the number of people who

KEY (CORRECT ANSWERS)

1.	B	11.	D
2.	C	12.	B
3.	A	13.	C
4.	D	14.	C
5.	B	15.	A
6.	A	16.	C
7.	B	17.	A
8.	B	18.	B
9.	C	19.	D
10.	A	20.	E

21. C
22. A
23. C
24. A
25. B

TEST 4

DIRECTIONS: Each question or incomplete statement is followed by several suggested answers or completions. Select the one that BEST answers the question or completes the statement. *PRINT THE LETTER OF THE CORRECT ANSWER IN THE SPACE AT THE RIGHT.*

Questions 1-5.

DIRECTIONS: Each of the sentences provided in Questions 1 through 5 may be:
   A. Incorrect due to improper spelling
   B. Incorrect due to improper punctuation
   C. Incorrect due to improper capitalization
   D. Correct

1. When you search the library's catalog online you can search by author, title, subject or, keyword. 1.____

2. The movie "Ghostbusters" is available on DVD or Blu-Ray in the library's audiovisual department. 2.____

3. The library hosts a group for writers that meets monthly and a children's story hour that meets weekly. 3.____

4. Reference librarians are best equipped to answer questions about the library's electronic resorces. 4.____

5. Library patrons can sign into their library account online to pay fines, rezerve books and check their due dates. 5.____

Questions 6-10.

DIRECTIONS: Questions 6 through 10 include sentences with one word underlined. Please select the word with the CLOSEST meaning to the underlined word.

6. The patron has <u>requested</u> that the book be held for an extra two days because she is on vacation. 6.____
   A. refused   B. asked   C. determined   D. stated

7. The Oak Creek Village Library participates in a <u>reciprocal</u> borrowing program in which it shares library materials with 25 other libraries. 7.____
   A. individual   B. restrictive
   C. collaborative   D. bibliographic

8. In libraries, books are assigned a call number based upon the book's <u>subject</u>. 8.____
   A. title   B. author   C. chronology   D. topic

15

9. Every year, the library director and board of directors review and update   9.____
   library policies.
   A. procedures   B. collections   C. events   D. affairs

10. Librarians at the Poplar Lane Library are sometimes asked to proctor official   10.____
    tests and exams.
    A. barter   B. supervise   C. process   D. create

Questions 11-15.

DIRECTIONS: In answering Questions 11 through 15, arrange the following names in alphabetical order as they would appear on the hold shelf of a library by matching the name in Column A with its order position in Column B.

Column A

11. Frey, James

12. Friend, Jayne

13. Frye, Jada

14. Friel, Jewel

15. Frillo, Juno

Column B

A. First
B. Second
C. Third
D. Fourth
E. Fifth

11.____
12.____
13.____
14.____
15.____

Questions 16-20.

DIRECTIONS: Questions 16 through 20 each consist of four call numbers in Column A and Column B. Compare the numbers listed in each column and use the following to provide your answer:
A. One call number in Column A and Column B are the same.
B. Two call numbers in Column A and Column B are the same.
C. Three call numbers in Column A and Column B are the same.
D. All four call numbers in Column A and Column B are the same.

Column A	Column B
16. 147.74CAL	147.74CAL
174.47LAC	174.44LAC
144.77LAL	177.44LAL
411.77CAC	477.11CAL

16.____

17. 467.09DAN	467.09DAN
469.07DAD	469.07DAD
460.79NAD	460.79NAD
468.32DAJ	468.23DAJ

17.____

18. 219.57KAR   219.57KAR   18._____
     215.97KAR   215.57KAR
     257.19RAR   257.19RAR
     275.19KAK   275.19KAK

19. 112.48PAU   112.58PAU   19._____
     112.85PUA   112.85PUA
     124.18PUL   124.18PUL
     142.85PAU   142.85PAA

20. 102.75CHR   102.75CHR   20._____
     175.27CRI   175.27CRI
     107.25CHR   107.25CHR
     157.22CRI   157.22CRI

21. Old Towne Library is hosting a speaking event and book signing with a   21._____
     well-known author. Seats are available for 120 people, but the author only has
     one hour to sign books afterward. If it takes about three minutes to sign each
     person's book, how many of the event's attendees will be able to participate in
     the book signing?
     A. All of them   B. 20   C. 100   D. 50

22. If Fleetwood Library owns a total of 1,000 DVDs (500 in the fiction section and   22._____
     500 in the non-fiction section), how many DVDs would the library have left if the
     library director decided to withdraw 120 fiction DVDs and 150 non-fiction DVDs,
     while simultaneously adding 75 fiction DVDs and 60 non-fiction DVDs?
     A. 730   B. 805   C. 865   D. 950

23. Tandy has been asked to create the schedule for the circulation staff at   23._____
     Morton Pass Library. The library is open from 10 A.M. to 9 P.M. Monday
     through Friday, from 10 A.M. to 5 P.M. on Saturday, and from 12 P.M. to 5 P.M.
     on Sunday. The library director requires that two staff members work at the
     desk during all hours of operation. What is the TOTAL number of hours Tandy
     will need to schedule staff for next week's schedule?
     A. 134   B. 55   C. 201   D. 68

24. The Boynton Canyon Library hosts a weekly book discussion group every   24._____
     Thursday night. If 8 people attended the group the first week of February, 11
     attended the second week, 7 attended the third week, and 10 attended the
     fourth week, what is the average number of attendees for the month of
     February?
     A. 9   B. 34   C. 10   D. 7

25. A library patron has $6.60 in fines on his library account. He returns five more books five days late and is charged $.15 a day for each book. The library does not let patrons check out library materials when the fines on their account exceed $10.00. Which of the following statements BEST describes the patron's current situation?
The patron
   A. has less than $10.00 in fines and can still check out library materials
   B. must pay at least $1.00 in fines before he can check out more library materials
   C. must pay at least $.60 in fines before he can check out more library materials
   D. must pay at least $.35 in fines before he can check out more library materials

25.____

KEY (CORRECT ANSWERS)

1.	B		11.	A
2.	C		12.	C
3.	D		13.	E
4.	A		14.	B
5.	A		15.	D
6.	B		16.	A
7.	C		17.	C
8.	D		18.	C
9.	A		19.	B
10.	B		20.	D

21.	B
22.	C
23.	A
24.	A
25.	D

EXAMINATION SECTION
TEST 1

DIRECTIONS: Each question or incomplete statement is followed by several suggested answers or completions. Select the one that BEST answers the question or completes the statement. *PRINT THE LETTER OF THE CORRECT ANSWER IN THE SPACE AT THE RIGHT.*

1. An employee requests a book which is not in the department library.
   Of the following, the MOST advisable course of action for you to take is to

   A. attempt to get the book for him by means of the department's affiliation with the public library
   B. explain that the book is not available from the department's library
   C. suggest that he try his local public library and give him a list of local libraries
   D. tell him where he may purchase the book and offer to make the purchase for him

   1.____

2. The catalog for the use of department employees has just been thoroughly checked and revised by a professional librarian. After trying to find the name of a book in the catalog, an employee tells you that he cannot find it.
   Of the following, the MOST advisable action for you to take FIRST is to

   A. call the public library for the exact title
   B. look it up in the catalog yourself
   C. look through the stacks for the book
   D. tell him you are sorry but the book is not in the department library

   2.____

3. You find that three pages are missing from one of the copies of a very popular book in the department library.
   Of the following, the MOST advisable action for you to take is to

   A. discard the book since its usefulness is now sharply curtailed
   B. order another copy of the book but keep the old copy until the new one is received
   C. report the fact to the head of the department and request further instructions
   D. type copies of the pages from another volume of the book and tape them in the appropriate place

   3.____

4. The department library is scheduled to close at 5 P.M. It is now 4:55, and an employee reading a book shows no signs of leaving.
   Of the following, the MOST advisable action for you to take is to

   A. tell him it is time to leave
   B. tell him the time and ask him if he wishes to borrow the book
   C. turn the lights off and on, indirectly suggesting that he leave
   D. wait until he decides to leave

   4.____

5. The dealer from whom you have been buying books for the department library has informed you that henceforth he can give you only a fifteen percent instead of a twenty percent discount.
   Of the following, the MOST advisable course of action for you to take FIRST is to

   5.____

A. accept the fifteen percent discount
B. inform the head of your department
C. investigate the discount given by other book dealers
D. order directly from the publishers

6. Your supervisor is a professional librarian and is responsible for the selection of material to be added to the department library in which you are an employee. Shortly after you start on the job, an employee of the department brings you a written request to have several books of his choice added to the library.
Of the following, the MOST advisable course of action for you to take is to

    A. order the books immediately
    B. pass the suggestion along to your supervisor
    C. refuse to accept his suggestion
    D. tell him that he will have to buy the books

7. You object to your supervisor's plan to change the system in the department library from closed to open stacks.
Of the following, the MOST advisable course of action for you to take is to

    A. ask other members of the staff to support your objections
    B. await further instructions and then do as you are told
    C. discuss your objections with your supervisor
    D. send a brief report of your objections to the department head

8. Two weeks after you begin working in the department library, you learn that books in library bindings last twice as long as those with the publishers' bindings.
Of the following, the MOST advisable course of action for you to follow is to

    A. buy only paperbound books
    B. have all new books put in library bindings
    C. put in library bindings only rare editions
    D. put in library bindings only those books likely to get hard use

9. Your superior is away on an official trip. You have been asked to type and e-mail several hundred letters before he returns. Just as you begin the job, the computer breaks down.
Of the following, the MOST advisable course of action for you to take is to

    A. arrange to have the computer serviced as soon as possible
    B. write the letters by hand
    C. postpone the job until after your supervisor returns
    D. write to your supervisor for advice

10. Your supervisor in the department library is out for the day. You receive a telephone call from another city department asking if they may borrow one of the books in your library.
Of the following, the MOST advisable action for you to take FIRST is to tell the department

    A. that books are not permitted out of the department
    B. that you will check and call back the next day
    C. to send a representative to inquire the next day
    D. to write a letter to the department head

11. Two months have passed since the head of the department has borrowed one of the books in the department library. Of the following, the MOST advisable action for you to take is to

    A. ask the department head if he wishes to keep the book out longer
    B. leave a note for the department head telling him that the book should be returned immediately
    C. wait another month and then write the book off as lost
    D. wait until you receive another request for the book

12. Your supervisor tells you that he would like to have all old book cards replaced, all torn pages mended, and the books put in good condition in all other respects by the following day. You know that this is an impossible task.
    Of the following, the MOST advisable course of action for you to take is to

    A. attempt to finish as much of the job as possible
    B. explain the difficulties involved to the supervisor and await further instruction
    C. ignore the request since it is completely unreasonable
    D. make a complaint to the head of the department

13. The library in which you work has received about fifty new books. These books must be cataloged, but you have had no experience in this type of work. However, you have been told that a professional librarian will join the staff in about six weeks.
    Of the following, the MOST advisable course of action for you to take in the meantime is to

    A. close the library for a week and try to do the cataloging yourself
    B. lend the books only to those who can get special permission
    C. let the users take the books even though they are not cataloged
    D. put all the books in storage until they can be cataloged

14. The hospital library in which you work has a large back-log of books that need to be mended. You are unable to do more than a small part of the job by yourself. One of the patients in the hospital has done book binding and mending. He offers to help you because he sees the need for doing the job and because he wants something to do with his hands.
    Of the following, the MOST advisable course of action for you to take is to

    A. accept his offer on condition that the doctor approves
    B. ask him to push the book cart around the wards so you will be free to do the mending
    C. refuse his offer
    D. write a letter to his former employer to find out whether he is a good bookbinder

15. You accidentally spill a glass of water over an open book.
    Of the following, the MOST advisable action for you to take FIRST in most cases is to

    A. discard the book to prevent the water from spoiling other material
    B. hang the book up by its binding
    C. press the covers together to squeeze out the water
    D. separate the wet pages with blotters

16. In mending a book, you overturn a jar of glue on a new book.
Of the following, the MOST advisable action for you to take FIRST is to

    A. allow the glue to harden so that it may be peeled off
    B. attempt to wipe off the glue with any clean scrap paper
    C. discard the book to prevent other materials from being spoiled
    D. report the incident immediately to your supervisor

17. Of the following, the situation LEAST likely to result in injury to books is one in which

    A. all books support each other standing upright
    B. short books are placed between tall ones
    C. the books are as close together as possible
    D. the books lean against the sides of the shelves

18. Of the following, a damp cloth may BEST be used to clean a cloth book cover that has been coated with

    A. benzene   B. gold leaf
    C. turpentine   D. varnish

19. Decay of leather bindings may be MOST effectively delayed by

    A. a short tanning period
    B. air conditioning
    C. rubbing periodically with a damp cloth
    D. treatment with heat

20. When paste is used to mend a page, it is MOST desirable that the page should then be

    A. aired   B. heated   C. pressed   D. sprayed

21. A book that is perfectly clean but has been used by someone with chicken pox can probably BEST be handled by

    A. burning, followed by proper disposal of the ashes
    B. forty-eight hour exposure to ultraviolet light
    C. keeping it out of circulation for six months
    D. treating it the same as any other book

22. The BEST combination of temperature and humidity for books is temperature _____ degrees, humidity _____.

    A. 50-60; 20-30%   B. 60-70; 10-20%
    C. 60-70; 50-60%   D. 70-80; 70-80%

23. When a new book is received, it is LEAST important to keep a record of the

    A. author's name
    B. cost of the book
    C. number of pages
    D. source from which it was obtained

24. You have just received from the publisher a new book for the department library, but you find that the binding is torn.
Of the following, the MOST advisable action for you to take is to

   A. mend the binding and take no further action
   B. mend the binding but claim a price discount
   C. report the damage to the department head
   D. send the book back to the publisher

24.____

25. Of the following, a characteristic of MOST photographic charging systems is that

   A. book cards are not used
   B. charging is done by one person
   C. date due is stamped on borrower's card
   D. transaction cards are not used

25.____

KEY (CORRECT ANSWERS)

1.	A	11.	A
2.	B	12.	B
3.	D	13.	C
4.	B	14.	A
5.	C	15.	D
6.	B	16.	B
7.	C	17.	A
8.	D	18.	D
9.	A	19.	B
10.	B	20.	C

21. D
22. C
23. C
24. D
25. B

TEST 2

DIRECTIONS: Each question or incomplete statement is followed by several suggested answers or completions. Select the one that BEST answers the question or completes the statement. *PRINT THE LETTER OF THE CORRECT ANSWER IN THE SPACE AT THE RIGHT.*

1. In a card catalog, a reference from one subject heading to another is MOST commonly called a(n) _____ reference. 1.____

    A. cross B. direct C. primary D. indirect

2. A book which is shortened by omission of detail but which retains the general sense of the original is called a(n) 2.____

    A. compendium B. manuscript
    C. miniature D. abridgment

3. An anonymous book is a 3.____

    A. book published before 1500
    B. book whose author is unknown
    C. copy which is defective
    D. work that is out of print

4. All the letters, figures, and symbols assigned to a book to indicate its location on library shelves comprise the _____ number. 4.____

    A. call B. Cutter C. index D. inventory

5. The term *format* does NOT refer to a book's 5.____

    A. binding B. size
    C. theme D. typography

6. The term *card catalog* USUALLY refers to a 6.____

    A. catalog consisting of loose-leaf pages upon which the cards are pasted
    B. catalog in which entries are on separate cards arranged in a definite order
    C. catalog of the cards available from the Library of Congress
    D. record on cards of the works which have been weeded out of the library collection

7. The term *circulation record* USUALLY refers to a record of 7.____

    A. daily attendance
    B. the books borrowed
    C. the most popular books
    D. the books out on interlibrary loan

8. Reading shelves USUALLY involves checking the shelves to see that all the books 8.____

    A. are in the correct order
    B. are suitable for the library's patrons
    C. are there
    D. have been cataloged correctly

9. In an alphabetical catalog of book titles and authors' names, the name *de Santis* would be filed

    A. after *DeWitt*
    B. after *Sanders*
    C. before AND THEN THERE WERE NONE
    D. before *Deutsch*

10. In typing, the Shift key on the computer keyboard is used to

    A. change the font size
    B. indent a line of text
    C. type numbers
    D. type capitals

11. The abbreviation e.g. means *most nearly*

    A. as follows
    B. for example
    C. refer to
    D. that is

12. The abbreviation ff. means *most nearly*

    A. and following pages
    B. formerly
    C. frontispiece
    D. the end

13. The abbreviation ibid, means *most nearly*

    A. consult the index
    B. in the same place
    C. see below
    D. turn the page

14. *Ex libris* is a Latin phrase meaning

    A. former librarian
    B. from the books
    C. without charge
    D. without liberty

15. An expurgated edition of a book is one which

    A. contains many printing errors
    B. includes undesirable passages
    C. is not permitted in public libraries
    D. omits objectionable material

16. The re-charging of a book to a borrower is USUALLY called

    A. fining
    B. processing
    C. reissue
    D. renewal

17. A sheet of paper that is pierced with holes is

    A. borated
    B. collated
    C. perforated
    D. serrated

18. *Glossary* means *most nearly* a(n)

    A. dictionary of selected terms in a particular book or field
    B. list of chapter headings in the order in which they appear in a book
    C. section of the repairing division which coats books with a protective lacquer
    D. alphabetical table of the contents of a book

19. *Accessioning* means *most nearly*

    A. acquiring books
    B. arranging books for easy access
    C. donating books as gifts
    D. listing books in the order of purchase

20. *Bookplate* means *most nearly*

    A. a label in a book showing who owns it
    B. a metal device for holding books upright
    C. a rounded zinc surface upon which a page is printed
    D. the flat part of the binding of a book

21. *Thesaurus* means *most nearly* a book which

    A. contains instructions on how to prepare a thesis
    B. contains words grouped according to similarity of meaning
    C. describes the techniques of dramatic acting
    D. gives quotations from well-known works of literature

22. *Salacious* means *most nearly*

    A. careful   B. delicious   C. lewd   D. salty

23. *Pseudonym* means *most nearly*

    A. false report   B. fictitious name
    C. libelous statement   D. psychic phenomenon

24. *Gamut* means *most nearly* a(n)

    A. bookworm   B. simpleton
    C. vagrant   D. entire range

25. *Monograph* means *most nearly* a

    A. machine for duplicating typewritten material by means of a stencil
    B. picture reproduced on an entire page of a manuscript
    C. single chart used to represent statistical data
    D. systematic treatise on a particular subject

KEY (CORRECT ANSWERS)

1. A
2. D
3. B
4. A
5. C

6. B
7. B
8. A
9. D
10. D

11. B
12. A
13. B
14. B
15. D

16. D
17. C
18. A
19. D
20. A

21. B
22. C
23. B
24. D
25. D

TEST 3

DIRECTIONS: Each question or incomplete statement is followed by several suggested answers or completions. Select the one that BEST answers the question or completes the statement. *PRINT THE LETTER OF THE CORRECT ANSWER IN THE SPACE AT THE RIGHT.*

Questions 1-15.

DIRECTIONS: Questions 1 through 15 are to be answered SOLELY on the basis of the information contained in the following passage.

Machines may be useful for bibliographic purposes, but they will be useful only if we study the bibliographic requirements to be met and the machines available, in terms of each job which needs to be done. Many standard tools now available are more efficient than high-speed machines if the machines are used as gadgets rather than as the mechanical elements of well-considered systems.

It does not appear impossible for us to learn to think in terms of scientific management to such an extent that we may eventually be able to do much of the routine part of bibliographic work mechanically with greater efficiency, both in terms of cost per unit of service and in terms of management of the intellectual content of literature. There are many bibliographic tasks which will probably not be done mechanically in the near future because the present tools appear to present great advantages over any machine in sight; for example, author bibliography done on the electronic machines would appear to require almost as much work in instructing the machine as is required to look in an author catalog. The major field of usefulness of the machines would appear to be that of subject bibliography, and particularly in research rather than quick reference jobs.

Machines now available or in sight cannot answer a quick reference question either as fast or as economically as will consultation of standard reference works such as dictionaries, encyclopedias, or almanacs, nor would it appear worthwhile to instruct a machine and run the machine to pick out one recent book or "any recent book" in a broad subject field. It would appear, therefore, that high-speed electronic or electrical machinery may be used for bibliographic purposes only in research institutions, at least for the next five or ten years, and their use will probably be limited to research problems in those institutions. It seems quite probable that during the next decade electronic machines, including the Rapid Selector, which was designed with bibliographic purposes in mind, will find application in administrative, office, and business uses to a much greater extent than they will in bibliographic operations.

The shortcomings of machines used as gadgets have been stressed in this paper. Nevertheless, the use of machines for bibliographic purposes is developing, and it is developing rapidly. It appears quite certain that several of the machines and mechanical devices can now perform certain of the routine operations involved in bibliographic work more accurately and more efficiently than these operations can be performed without them.

At least one machine, the Rapid Selector, appears potentially capable of performing higher orders of bibliographic work than we have been able to perform in the past, if and when we learn: (a) what is really needed for the advancement of learning in the way of bibliographic services; and (b) how to utilize the machine efficiently.

There is no magic in machines as such. There will be time-lag in their application, just as there was with the typewriter. The speed and efficiency in handling the mechanical part of bibliographic work, which will determine the point of diminishing returns, depend in large measure on how long it will be before we approach these problems from the point of view of scientific management.

This report cannot solve the problem of bibliographic organization. Machines alone cannot solve the problem. We need to develop systems of handling the mass of bibliographic material, but such systems cannot be developed until we discover and establish our objectives, our plans, our standards, our methods and controls, within the framework of each situation. This may take twenty years or it may take one hundred, but it will come. The termination of how long the time-lag will be rests upon our time-lag in gathering objective information upon which scientific management of literature can be based.

1. On the basis of the above passage, machines will *probably* be MOST useful in

    A. determining the cost per unit of service
    B. quick reference jobs
    C. subject bibliography
    D. title cataloging

2. On the basis of the above passage, the Rapid Selector will *probably* be LEAST used during the next ten years in

    A. administration
    B. bibliographic work
    C. business
    D. office work

3. It may be inferred from the above passage that is is NOT practical to use machines to do author bibliography because

    A. experienced machine operators are not available
    B. more than one machine is needed for such a task
    C. the results obtained from a machine are unreliable
    D. too much work is involved in instructing the machine

4. On the basis of the above passage, one of the criteria of efficiency is the

    A. amount of work required
    B. cost per unit of service
    C. net cost of service
    D. number of machines available

5. On the basis of the above passage, the LEAST efficient of the following for quick reference jobs are

    A. bibliographies
    B. dictionaries
    C. encyclopedias
    D. machines

6. On the basis of the above passage, in the next few years, high-speed electronic machinery will probably be used for bibliographic purposes only by

    A. civil engineers
    B. institutions of higher education
    C. publishers
    D. research institutions

7. On the basis of the above passage, the Rapid Selector was designed for use in handling

   A. bibliographic operations
   B. computing problems
   C. photographic reproduction
   D. standard reference works

8. On the basis of the above passage, progress on the development of machines to do bibliographic tasks has reached the point at which

   A. all present tools have become obsolete
   B. certain jobs are better performed with machines than without them
   C. machines are as efficient in doing quick reference jobs as in doing special research jobs
   D. machines are no longer regarded as being too expensive

9. The one of the following which is NOT stated by the above passage to be essential in developing ways of handling bibliographic material is

   A. discovering methods and controls
   B. establishing objectives
   C. establishing standards
   D. obtaining historical data

10. The above passage indicates that machines alone will NOT be able to solve the problem of

    A. bibliographic organization
    B. reference work
    C. scientific management
    D. system analysis

11. On the basis of the above passage, the viewpoint of scientific management is essential in

    A. developing the mechanical handling of bibliographic work
    B. operating the Rapid Selector
    C. repairing electronic machines
    D. showing that people are always superior to machines in bibliographic work

12. On the basis of the above passage, there are machines in existence which

    A. are particularly useful for statistical analysis in library work
    B. are the result of scientific management of bibliographic work
    C. have not been efficiently utilized for bibliographic work
    D. may be installed in a medium-sized library

13. On the basis of the above passage, the scientific management of literature awaits the

    A. assembling of objective information
    B. compilation of new reference books
    C. development of more complex machines
    D. development of simplified machinery

14. Based on the above passage, it may be INFERRED that the author's attitude toward the use of machines in bibliographic work is that they 14._____

    A. have limited usefulness at the present time
    B. will become useful only if scientific management is applied
    C. will probably always be restricted to routine operations
    D. will probably never be useful

15. The author of the above passage believes that high-speed machines are BEST adapted to bibliographic work when they are used 15._____

    A. as gadgets
    B. in place of standard reference works
    C. to perform complex operations
    D. to perform routine operations

Questions 16-25.

DIRECTIONS: Questions 16 through 25 deal with the classification of non-fiction books according to the Dewey Classification as outlined below. For each book listed, print in the space on the right the letter in front of the class to which it belongs.

Classification

16. Ernst. WORDS: ENGLISH ROOTS AND HOW THEY GROW	A.	000 General Works	16._____	
17. Faulkner. FROM VERSAILLES TO THE NEW DEAL	B.	100 Philosophy	17._____	
18. Fry. CHINESE ART	C.	200 Religion	18._____	
19. Kant. CRITIQUE OF PURE REASON	D.	300 Social Science	19._____	
20. Millikan. THE ELECTRON	E.	400 Philology	20._____	
21. Morgan. THEORY OF THE GENE	F.	500 Pure Science	21._____	
22. Raine. THE YEAR ONE; POEMS	G.	600 Applied Science, Useful Arts	22._____	
23. Richards. PRINCIPLES OF LITERARY CRITICISM	H.	700 Fine Arts	23._____	
24. Steinberg. BASIC JUDAISM	I.	800 Literature, Belleslettres	24._____	
25. Strachey. QUEEN VICTORIA	J.	900 History, Biography	25._____	

KEY (CORRECT ANSWERS)

1. C
2. B
3. D
4. B
5. D

6. D
7. A
8. B
9. D
10. A

11. A
12. C
13. A
14. A
15. D

16. E
17. J
18. H
19. B
20. F

21. F
22. I
23. I
24. C
25. J

———

EXAMINATION SECTION

TEST 1

DIRECTIONS: Each question or incomplete statement is followed by several suggested answers or completions. Select the one that BEST answers the question or completes the statement. *PRINT THE LETTER OF THE CORRECT ANSWER IN THE SPACE AT THE RIGHT.*

1. The process of building or improving a collection of library materials is known as
   A. collection development
   B. cataloging
   C. reader's advisory
   D. collection sourcing

   1.____

2. While working at the library circulation desk, a library assistant encounters a patron who is angry because a book he checked out is showing up as overdue when he is certain he has returned it. The patron begins yelling at her and, although she is maintaining a calm tone and demeanor, she is beginning to feel uncomfortable with the interaction. What should she do next?
   A. Call the police
   B. Call for backup from the person in charge
   C. Ban the patron from the library
   D. Remove the book from the patron's account

   2.____

3. In recent years, many libraries have adopted _____ technology, which uses radio waves that allow patrons to check out several items at once without opening or scanning them.
   A. Bluetooth
   B. Cloud
   C. RFID
   D. LCD

   3.____

4. The American Library Association defines _____ as "documents which define the scope of a library's existing collections, plan for the continuing development of resources, identify collection strengths and outline the relationship between selection philosophy and the institution's goals, general selection criteria and intellectual freedom."
   A. card catalog records
   B. cataloging manuals
   C. reader's advisory policies
   D. collection development policies

   4.____

5. A library assistant is sometimes asked to go to a section of the stacks to make sure each item is in the proper order based upon call number. This is an important aspect of stack management known as
   A. shelf-reading
   B. copy cataloging
   C. book browsing
   D. shelf-shifting

   5.____

6. While libraries once used card catalogs to share library holdings information with library users, today libraries use _____ to do this.
   A. aggregator-neutral records (ANR)
   B. SQL cloud databases
   C. acquisition sections (AS)
   D. online public access catalogs (OPACs)

   6.____

7. Which of the following is NOT true of the Dewey Decimal Classification system?
   A. It is composed of 10 classes
   B. It is the classification system used in all academic libraries
   C. It is hierarchical in nature
   D. Each class in the system is composed of ten divisions

8. Which of the following is used by libraries to manage Internet access and comply with the Children Internet Protection Act?
   A. Anti-virus software
   B. Electronic reserves
   C. Internet filters
   D. OCLC database

9. While helping a patron check out, a library assistant notices that the patron is checking out one of her favorite books. What should the assistant do in this situation? She should
   A. comment on the book to create a sense of goodwill between her and the patron
   B. not comment on the book but make a mental note of the patron's selection so she can bring it up in future conversations
   C. comment on the book and recommend a few other books the patron might like based on his selection
   D. not comment on the book to maintain the patron's privacy

10. In the Dewey Decimal system, books related to the arts receive call numbers between _____ and _____.
    A. 700; 799
    B. 600; 699
    C. 100; 199
    D. 300; 399

11. While shelving books, a library assistant notices a patron walking through the stacks looking for a book. What should she do in this situation? She should
    A. stop shelving, greet the patron and ask if she needs help
    B. continue shelving books unless the patron requests her assistance
    C. smile at the patron and then, when she's done shelving, ask the patron if she needs assistance
    D. avoid making eye contact with the patron to ensure the patron's privacy

12. While he is working at the reference desk, a library assistant is asked by a patron where to find books about pets. How should he respond?
    A. By telling the patron that books about pets are located in the 630s
    B. By telling the patron that he can look up any book or subject on the catalog computer
    C. By asking the patron questions to determine more specifically what type of pet books the patron is looking for and then guiding him to them
    D. By calling a co-worker who is an avid pet lover to help the patron

13. Which call number would be MOST appropriate for a book about Zen Buddhism?
    A. 899.5
    B. 646.2
    C. 294.3
    D. 103.5

14. When a library assistant is helping a patron at the circulation desk, the patron asks to check out a reference book. The assistant knows that the library has a strict policy against checking out reference materials. What should she do in this situation?
    A. Ask the circulation manager if she can make an exception in this one case
    B. Recommend other options to the patron like photocopying the parts of the book the patron needs or finding a similar book in the circulating collection
    C. Tell the patron she is sorry but there is nothing she can do
    D. Tell the patron about the library's policy but agree to check the book out for him this one time

14.____

15. The Dewey Decimal system organizes items based upon
    A. title   B. subject
    C. publication date   D. author

15.____

16. When a library assistant calls a patron to inform him that a book he requested has arrived, the patron's wife answers and offers to take a message. What information should the assistant give to the patron's wife?
    A. "Your husband's copy of *The 4-Hour Work Week* has arrived, and it will be held for one week."
    B. "An item your husband requested has arrived, and if he wants more information, he should call the library directly."
    C. "Your husband's copy of *The 4-Hour Work Week* has arrived, and we expect his copy of *The 4-Hour Body* to arrive tomorrow."
    D. "A book has arrived for your husband, and we will hold it for one week."

16.____

17. In a library, the act of adding an item to the library catalog, including a bibliographic description and classification, is known as
    A. cataloging   B. indexing
    C. bibliographic processing   D. descriptive linking

17.____

18. While checking in items at the circulation desk, a library assistant comes across a book with very loose binding and several pages falling out. He also notices that a patron has a hold on this particular title. What should he do?
    He should check the book in and then
    A. put it on hold for the patron
    B. follow his library's procedure for sending a book to the bindery for repair, as well as request a copy of the book from another library for the patron waiting
    C. call the patron who is waiting for the book and ask her whether she would rather take the book as it is or wait until it is repaired
    D. withdraw the book from the catalog and throw it away

18.____

19. On occasions where it is necessary for library staff to make a notation in a book, this should be done
    A. with a bold marker to ensure that the notation is seen
    B. with a pen that matches the color of the book's font
    C. lightly, with a soft pencil to prevent any indentations
    D. with a typed label created in a labelmaker

19.____

20. Which of the following is TRUE about the proper procedure for handling audio-visual materials such as CDs, DVDs and Blu-ray discs?
    A. They should only be handled by touching the edges and the center hole
    B. They can be touched anywhere as long as they are cleaned regularly
    C. They should never be touched unless you are wearing gloves
    D. Any visible scratches should be buffed out with a moist paper towel

20.____

21. Which of the following behaviors represents the proper use of a photocopier in a library?
    A. Photocopying a very old, rare book
    B. Photocopying a book by laying it flat on the glass and pressing down on the spine so you can copy two pages at a time
    C. Photocopying a book one page at a time by placing half of the book on the glass and supporting the rest of the book with your hand
    D. Photocopying the loose pages of a book with a broken spine just in case the pages go missing

21.____

22. A library's _____ includes books and other items that are housed separately from the main collection due to their rarity, value, condition, subject or history.
    A. serial collection   B. archives
    C. reference section   D. special collections

22.____

23. When Mr. Buckley, a regular patron at Elm Park Library, registers for a library program called "Surviving Divorce," a library assistant says to his co-worker, "Did you see that Mr. Buckley registered for the divorce program: No wonder I haven't seen Mrs. Buckley around lately." Considering that he is a professional library worker, what is wrong with the assistant's comment?
    A. He is impinging upon the patron's right to intellectual freedom
    B. He is not fulfilling his responsibility to maintain the patron's confidentiality
    C. He is speculating about the patron's relationship without any concrete facts
    D. He is slandering the patron and could be sued for defamation

23.____

24. While a library assistant is working at the circulation desk, a distraught patron comes to the desk with a stack of books and explains that he forgot his library card at home but really needs the books for a paper he is working on that is due tomorrow. The patron is worried because the library is closing in ten minutes, and he won't have time to go home and get his card. What should the assistant do in this situation?
    A. Ask the patron for a photo I.D. so she can pull up his account manually and check out the books

24.____

B. Ask the patron for his name so she can pull up his account manually and check out the books
C. Ask the patron for his library card number so she can pull up his account manually and check out the books
D. Tell the patron that there is nothing she can do and that if he wants the books he will have to return tomorrow

25. Most libraries in the United States use either the Dewey Decimal system or the _____ Classification system for classifying and organizing library materials.   25._____
    A. Colon
    B. Library of Congress
    C. Bliss
    D. Universal Decimal

KEY (CORRECT ANSWERS)

1.	A		11.	A
2.	B		12.	C
3.	C		13.	C
4.	D		14.	B
5.	A		15.	B
6.	D		16.	D
7.	B		17.	A
8.	C		18.	B
9.	D		19.	C
10.	A		20.	A

21.	C
22.	D
23.	B
24.	A
25.	B

TEST 2

DIRECTIONS: Each question or incomplete statement is followed by several suggested answers or completions. Select the one that BEST answers the question or completes the statement. *PRINT THE LETTER OF THE CORRECT ANSWER IN THE SPACE AT THE RIGHT.*

1. Which of the following is TRUE of caring for water-damaged books?　　1.____
   A. All types of books can be air-dried with good results
   B. Wet books should never be laid flat to air-dry because it promotes mold growth
   C. Paper towels tend to further damage books and should not be used to dry wet books
   D. Water-damaged books with glossy pages, leather or parchment should be immediately frozen

2. Public libraries typically require a _____ for library card registration.　　2.____
   A. current photo ID that includes the individual's name and address
   B. current photo ID and three personal references
   C. background and credit check
   D. birth certificate or Social Security card

3. Although library directors are typically the top authority in a library, most libraries are ultimately controlled by the　　3.____
   A. taxpayers
   B. board of trustees
   C. reference department
   D. technical services department

4. All of the following are functions of the Technical Services Department EXCEPT　　4.____
   A. cataloging
   B. processing
   C. acquisitions
   D. reader's advisory

5. A(n) _____ is a software program used by libraries to automate functions such as cataloging, circulation, serials, acquisitions and the online catalog for library patrons.　　5.____
   A. online public access catalog (OPAC)
   B. open source reporting system (OSRS)
   C. integrated library system (ILS)
   D. multiuser automated database (MAD)

6. While working at the reference desk, a library assistant gets caught in a lengthy conversation with a patron about his favorite author and why his first book is better than his second book. The assistant can tell the patron is lonely and looking for someone to talk to, but other patrons are also waiting for her help. What should she do in this situation?　　6.____
   She should
   A. continue talking to the patron while giving him behavioral clues, like looking at the clock, to suggest she needs to end the conversation

B. be blunt with the patron and tell him he is taking up too much of her time, otherwise he will continue to do so in the future
C. politely tell the patron she has to help the other patrons in line, but suggest that he participate in some of the library's clubs and events where he can talk to others who share his love of books
D. tell the patron to wait a minute, quickly help the other patrons in line, and then return to the conversation so as not to be rude

7. In the Library of Congress Classification system, the main classes are designated by
   A. letters of the alphabet
   B. special characters
   C. a three-digit code
   D. the author's last name

7.____

8. A library assistant works in the acquisitions unit and is asked by the director to order a replacement for a damaged book that was published in 1979. While searching for the book, he realizes that it is out-of-print. What should he do in this situation?
   A. Tell the director he can't order it
   B. Order it through a retailer, like Amazon, that often carries out-of-print items
   C. Order it through a wholesaler, like Baker & Taylor, that often carries out-of-print items
   D. Offer to buy it from another library that owns it

8.____

9. Who is typically the final decision maker when it comes to collection development in a library?
   A. The technical services manager
   B. The acquisition assistant
   C. The head reference librarian
   D. The library director

9.____

10. While working at the reference desk, a library assistant is approached by a patron who complains that another patron is talking very loudly on her cellphone in a quiet reading area. When the assistant asks the patron if she can take her call outside, the patron refuses and continues talking. How should the assistant handle this situation?
    She should
    A. forcibly confiscate the cellphone from the patron
    B. return to the reference desk and tell the patron who complained that she's sorry but there is nothing else she can do
    C. call her manager or the library director and have him or her ask the patron to take the call outside; if the patron still refuses, they can call the police
    D. grab the patron by the arm and escort her out of the building

10.____

11. All of the following are examples of e-resources EXCEPT
    A. microforms
    B. databases
    C. web resource links
    D. streaming media

11.____

12. Which call number would be MOST appropriate for a travel guide about Hawaii?
    A. 919.69
    B. 747.13
    C. 316.45
    D. 103.25

12.____

13. Public libraries receive most of their funding from which of the following sources?   13._____
    A. Individual donations
    B. State and local government
    C. Corporate donations
    D. Endowments

14. When processing books, library workers should always make sure to   14._____
    A. use a ballpoint pen to mark them
    B. attach notes to them with paperclips or rubber bands
    C. stack them with the smallest ones on the bottom and the biggest ones on the top
    D. use plain, acid-free paper for place markers or notes

15. Which of the following is NOT a fundamental characteristic of all public libraries?   15._____
    A. They are voluntary in nature, unlike public schools
    B. They provide most services free of charge
    C. They are open to most groups, except groups that are known to be discriminatory or controversial
    D. They are established by state law

16. While an assistant is working at the reference desk, a patron approaches her and asks her to help him on the computer. The patron had been working on a research paper when the computer crashed. He believes he might have lost half of his work, but he is hoping the assistant can help him access the work he lost. She follows the patron to his computer to see what she can do, but she is unable to figure out how to access the lost information. What should she say in this circumstance?   16._____
    A. "I'm sorry, but I haven't been able to find your lost work so far. Let me contact our IT specialist and see if she has any suggestions."
    B. "I haven't found your lost information, but I'm 100% positive it's here. So don't worry, I will definitely find it for you."
    C. "No one has ever had this problem with this computer before. What were you doing before it crashed?"
    D. "There's nothing I can do. You should have saved it more frequently."

17. Which of the following is TRUE of the Library of Congress Classification (LCC) system as compared to the Dewey Decimal Classification (DDC) system?   17._____
    A. The LCC system does not use cutter numbers, whereas the DDC system does
    B. The LCC system has more numbers and more specific classes than the DDC
    C. LCC call numbers are usually longer than DDC call numbers of the same specificity
    D. The LCC system tends to be easier to browse from a subject searcher's perspective

18. Which of the following BEST describes MARC formats?　　　　　　　　　　　　　　　　　18.____
    A. A set of cataloging rules　　　　B. A cataloging code
    C. A computer system　　　　　　D. A set of mark-up protocols

19. While working at the reference desk, an assistant receives a call from a patron who　　19.____
    wants more information on a special display that is set up in the Youth Services
    Department. How should he handle this request?
    He should
    A. tell the patron to hold and transfer her to Youth Services
    B. tell the patron everything he knows about the display and then suggest
       that if the patron wants to know more, she should call back and enter the
       extension for Youth Services
    C. tell the patron that he is going to transfer her to the librarian on-duty in
       Youth Services. He should also give the patron his name and extension
       just in case the patron gets disconnected
    D. take a message and tell the patron he will have the librarian in charge of
       the display call her back when she comes in for her next shift tomorrow

20. Which of the following is TRUE about the application of copyright law in　　　　　　　20.____
    libraries?
    A. The first sale doctrine allows libraries to lend books and other resources
       that are copyrighted
    B. Fair use frees libraries from any liability or responsibility when it comes to
       copyright regulations
    C. Copyright law prohibits libraries from reproducing copyrighted works for
       users with disabilities
    D. Libraries are not allowed to reproduce copyrighted works, even if it's for
       preservation and replacement purposes

21. Which of the following behaviors BEST demonstrates the American Library　　　　　21.____
    Association's "Poor People's Policy"?
    A. Asking a homeless patron not to sleep in the library because it makes
       other patrons uncomfortable
    B. Requiring proof of address for library card registration
    C. Hiring a security guard in an attempt to balance the need for open access
       with the need for safety
    D. Removing fees and overdue charges that can act as an access barrier to
       economically challenged patrons

22. In the Library of Congress Classification system, a book about philosophy　　　　　　22.____
    would be in a class designated by _____, whereas in the Dewey Decimal
    Classification system, it would be in a class designated by
    A. the number 200; the letter A　　　　B. the number 100; the letter B
    C. the letter A; the number 200　　　　D. the letter B; the number 100

23. An assistant is helping a patron who needs a book as soon as possible for a research project. The book, however, is already checked out to another patron and is not owned by any other libraries. What action should the assistant take?
    A. None; there is nothing he can do in this circumstance
    B. He should recall the book, which will require the patron who has it checked out to return it sooner
    C. He should place a hold on the book in hopes that the patron who has it checked out will realize that someone else is waiting for it and return it sooner
    D. He should call the patron who has it checked out and request that she return it immediately

23.____

24. Which of the following technologies is being adopted by many libraries as an alternative to barcodes?
    A. Accession records
    B. MARC records
    C. RFID tags
    D. RLG sensors

24.____

25. While an assistant is working at the circulation desk, a patron approaches him with a book she would like to check out but tells him she is from out of town and only has a library card from her own library. Which library program should he introduce the patron to?
    A. Interlibrary loan
    B. Reciprocal borrowing
    C. Document delivery
    D. Homebound services

25.____

KEY (CORRECT ANSWERS)

1.	D		11.	A
2.	A		12.	A
3.	B		13.	B
4.	D		14.	D
5.	C		15.	C
6.	C		16.	A
7.	A		17.	B
8.	B		18.	D
9.	D		19.	C
10.	C		20.	A

21.	D
22.	D
23.	B
24.	C
25.	B

TEST 3

DIRECTIONS: Each question or incomplete statement is followed by several suggested answers or completions. Select the one that BEST answers the question or completes the statement. *PRINT THE LETTER OF THE CORRECT ANSWER IN THE SPACE AT THE RIGHT.*

1. Which of the following terms is used to describe groups of libraries that participate in cooperative resource purchasing and sharing?
    A. Consortia
    B. Integrated library systems
    C. Public access systems
    D. Resource associations

   1.____

2. An assistant works in the Archives Department of an academic library and is often handling delicate historical books and documents. Which of the following behaviors should she NEVER engage in?
    A. Stacking oversized books on the bottom shelf so they don't protrude
    B. Using post-it notes to indicate when a book needs to be repaired
    C. Pulling books off the shelf from the spine with her fingers on the boards
    D. Washing her hands before handling library materials

   2.____

3. All of the following components are usually included in an integrated library system EXCEPT a(n) _____ module.
    A. acquisitions   B. serials   C. cataloging   D. marketing

   3.____

4. Which of the following is an example of proper library customer service over the phone?
    A. Telling a patron you are transferring him or her to another department before doing so
    B. Transferring a patron to another department without telling your co-worker what the patron's question is in order to save time
    C. Asking patrons to repeat their questions several times to ensure you answer them correctly
    D. Telling a patron you will call him back if you are too busy, but not specifying when since you don't know exactly when you'll have time

   4.____

5. Which of the following call numbers would be MOST appropriate for a book about holiday baking?
    A. 824.13HOL   B. 641.865HOL   C. 691.476BAK   D. 194.634MAK

   5.____

6. While working at the reference desk, a patron approaches an assistant to tell him that a book he is looking for is not on the shelf where it is supposed to be. The assistant pulls up the book's record in the online catalog and the catalog shows that the book should be on the shelf. What is the next step he should take in this situation?
    He should
    A. change the book's status to "missing"
    B. check the hold shelf for the book
    C. check the shelf himself to make sure the book is not there
    D. request a copy of the book from another library for the patron

   6.____

7. What aspect of collection management must be implemented when a section of a collection is full and there is no longer room for new titles in this section?
   A. Shelf reading
   B. Cataloging
   C. Shifting
   D. Reader's advisory

8. An assistant's manager gives him a list of items that need to be withdrawn from the library's collection to make room for new titles. This process is known as
   A. weeding   B. processing   C. shelf reading   D. deleting

9. Which of the following technologies is used by libraries, particularly newer academic libraries, to store large amounts of library items in a densely packed off-site location?
   A. Integrated library storage systems
   B. Automated storage and retrieval systems
   C. Consortia warehouses
   D. Radio frequency identification

10. All of the following have an impact on a library's public relations (PR) EXCEPT
    A. how employees answer the telephone
    B. how many items are improperly shelved
    C. the presence of clear and useful signage
    D. the number of members on the Board of Trustees

11. Which of the following is TRUE of trade publishers?
    A. The only publish non-fiction
    B. They sell to three primary markets: libraries, bookstores and wholesalers
    C. Their price is lower than other publishers due to mass sales
    D. They only publish fiction

12. Newspapers, magazines, newsletters and journals are all examples of _____ publications carried by libraries.
    A. database   B. mass-market   C. serial   D. trade

13. An assistant is helping a patron who is required to perform research using journals for a school paper. The paper must be on a topic related to the town's local history. What subcategory of journals would be MOST useful to this patron?
    A. Parochial journals
    B. Practical professional journals
    C. Primary and secondary research journals
    D. Nonspecialized journals for intellectuals

14. All of the following are typical methods for organizing journals and magazines in libraries EXCEPT
    A. alphabetically by title
    B. alphabetically by title within larger subject groupings
    C. alphabetically by publisher
    D. using the same classification system as books in the collection

14.____

15. An assistant is overseeing a shifting project in two major subject areas. What final step should he implement before the project is complete?
    A. The installation of bigger shelving units
    B. A thorough shelf reading
    C. The shifting of the subject sections immediately before and after the sections being shifted
    D. The creation of new shelving labels

15.____

16. While an assistant is working at the reference desk, a patron approaches him with a book she has been using for in-library research and asks him what she should do with the book now that she is done with it. What is the MOST appropriate response in this situation?
    He should
    A. tell the patron to return the book to the shelf where she found it
    B. tell the patron to put the book on one of the shelving carts located in the stacks
    C. tell the patron to put the book in the return drop at the circulation desk
    D. take the book from the patron and leave the reference desk to return the book to the shelf himself

16.____

17. While an assistant is working at the reference desk, a patron asks him for help locating a recent report published by the USDA. Where should he direct this patron?
    A. To the federal government's web portal USA.gov
    B. To the library's in-house government document archive
    C. To a Federal Depository Library Program (FDLP) library
    D. To their local village hall

17.____

18. If a patron asked for help finding a primary source for a school paper, which of the following would suffice?
    A. A television documentary on DVD
    B. An encyclopedia
    C. A historical diary found in the library's archives
    D. A peer-reviewed journal article

18.____

19. What is the PRIMARY factor used to determine whether an item is included in a library's archives or special collections?
    A. Whether the item is in high demand
    B. Whether it's owned by any other libraries
    C. Its age – only items over 30 years old should be included in these sections
    D. Whether it requires special care to ensure long-term preservation

19.____

20. An assistant was recently hired as a cataloging assistant and is cataloging her first 20.____
 book, which is a newly acquired title that is on the New York Times bestsellers
 list. Which of the following steps should she take FIRST?
 A. Decide upon a call number for the book
 B. Create an original record
 C. Search for an existing record she can copy
 D. Cover and label the book

Questions 21-25.

DIRECTIONS: In answering Questions 21 through 25, match the call number in Column A to its proper place on a library shelf in Column B.

Column A	Column B	
21. 654.1678BEA	A. First	21.____
22. 654.93ALG	B. Second	22.____
23. 645.1GOR	C. Third	23.____
24. 654.167CAL	D. Fourth	24.____
25. 654BEC	E. Fifth	

KEY (CORRECT ANSWERS)

1.	A		11.	B
2.	B		12.	C
3.	D		13.	A
4.	A		14.	C
5.	B		15.	B
6.	C		16.	B
7.	C		17.	A
8.	A		18.	C
9.	B		19.	D
10.	D		20.	C

21. D
22. E
23. A
24. C
25. B

TEST 4

DIRECTIONS: Each question or incomplete statement is followed by several suggested answers or completions. Select the one that BEST answers the question or completes the statement. *PRINT THE LETTER OF THE CORRECT ANSWER IN THE SPACE AT THE RIGHT.*

1. A library assistant is asked by her manager to give direction to a volunteer who is working at the library to fulfill community service requirements. The assistant has a lot of work to accomplish and is trying to decide which task would be the best to assign to the volunteer.
   Which of the following would be the BEST choice based upon the fact that the volunteer has no previous library experience and the assistant has little time to train him?
   Asking the volunteer to
   A. follow-up with a patron who left a message about a lost book
   B. re-shelve books that has just been repaired
   C. affix pre-made labels to items that have just been cataloged
   D. perform copy cataloging on newly received items

   1.____

2. A useful reference book has all of the following characteristics EXCEPT
   A. tiny typeface
   B. photographs and illustrations
   C. relevant cross-references
   D. an index with indented subheadings

   2.____

3. Which of the following is considered a secondary source?
   A. A journal article   B. An interview
   C. A manuscript   D. A photograph

   3.____

4. Which of the following is NOT a responsibility of a library's Board of Trustees?
   A. Appointing a library director
   B. Adopting an annual budget
   C. Creating written policies that govern library operations
   D. Identifying candidates and approving the selection of library staff

   4.____

5. While an assistant is working at the reference desk, a patron approaches her with his teenage son and tells her that he caught his son reading a book from the Young Adult collection that is inappropriate for someone his age. How should the assistant respond?
   A. By telling the patron he is out of line and is trying to impede upon First Amendment rights
   B. By telling the patron that if he doesn't like the library's collection, he is free to go elsewhere for books
   C. By apologizing to the patron and telling him she will remove the book from the collection immediately
   D. By telling the patron that she is sorry that he found the book upsetting and asking him if she can help and find something more acceptable for his son to read

   5.____

47

6. What database would be MOST helpful to a patron writing a paper for a master's level course in educational leadership?
    A. HeritageQuest
    B. LexisNexis
    C. ERIC
    D. Novelist Plus

7. While working in the Youth Services Department, an assistant notices that an older male patron is periodically staring at a child in a way that she finds suspicious. She is certain that this patron is not the child's parent or guardian because she saw the child enter the library with someone else. What should she do in this circumstance?
    A. Ask the patron to leave the department immediately, and if he doesn't, call the police
    B. Approach the patron and ask him if she can help him with anything. Regardless of his response, she should check in with the patron and ask if he needs help, to remind him of her presence. She can also keep an eye on him until he leaves the department.
    C. Ask her manager to come and address the situation. Serious situations should be left to the librarian in charge.
    D. Ask the patron directly why he is staring at the child and, depending on his response, take appropriate action, which may include police intervention or a lifetime ban from the library.

8. While she is working at the reference desk, an assistant is approached by a patron who asks for a book recommendation. The patron has just read the book *Big Magic* by Elizabeth Gilbert and wants to read something similar, but by a different author since he has already read all of Elizabeth Gilbert's books. The assistant is not familiar with this book and is at a loss for what to recommend. What should she do?
    A. Look up a description of the book, and if she still can't think of anything, enter the title into a database like Novelist Plus to see what it recommends.
    B. Recommend some of her own favorite books, even if they might not be similar.
    C. Call the reader's advisory librarian at home to ask for a recommendation.
    D. Tell the patron she is sorry but he will have to return to the library at another time for a recommendation.

9. Which, among the following library staff positions, typically has the MOST authority and would make operational decisions when a director or manager is not present?
    A. Library assistant
    B. Library page
    C. Reference librarian
    D. Administrative assistant

10. Which of the following databases would be MOST useful to a patron looking to access a newspaper article from 1998?
    A. Standard & Poor's Net Advantage
    B. General OneFile
    C. Gale Virtual Reference Library
    D. Novelist Plus

Questions 11-14.

DIRECTIONS: In answering Questions 11 through 14, match the library type in Column A with the description that MOST accurately describes it in Column B.

Column A   Column B

11. Special Library   A. A library that serves students in Grades K-12   11.____
12. Public Library   B. A library that serves a clientele in a particular niche   12.____
13. Academic Library   C. A library associated with a university or college   13.____
14. School Library   D. A library that serves members of a community   14.____

15. _____ refers to subject headings or terms selected by indexers to describe a concept and make searches easier and more relevant.   15.____
    A. Alt text   B. Abbreviated entry
    C. Keyword vocabulary   D. Controlled vocabulary

16. In most libraries, collection development is based on   16.____
    A. the preferences of its librarians
    B. directives from the American Library Association
    C. the priorities established in the library's Collection Development Policy
    D. the direction of the Board of Trustees

17. Which of the following is an example of a tertiary source?   17.____
    A. An encyclopedia   B. An interview
    C. A journal article   D. A letter

18. When you search a database using your own vocabulary, you are performing a _____ search.   18.____
    A. controlled vocabulary B. keyword
    C. accession   D. full text

19. Which of the following is the oldest and largest library association in the world?   19.____
    A. The International Association of University Libraries
    B. The American Library Association (ALA)
    C. The Online Computer Library Center (OCLC)
    D. The Medical Library Association

20. Which of the following is TRUE of RDA cataloging rules versus AACR2 cataloging rules?
    A. RDA generally avoids the use of abbreviations.
    B. RDA uses varied systems of measurement for an item's dimensions depending on the type of resource.
    C. RDA uses the term "heading" as opposed to AACR2's term "authorized access point."
    D. RDA does not differentiate between recording and transcribing elements.

20.____

Questions 21-25.

DIRECTIONS: In answering Questions 21 through 25, match the library book in Column A to the best fitting genre in Column B.

Column A

21. A factual book recounting the life of James Brown

22. A book set during the Holocaust with imaginary characters

23. A book set on an imaginary planet

24. A factual book about the American healthcare system

25. A book written by Nelson Mandela about his own life

Column B

A. Autobiography
B. Science fiction
C. Non-fiction
D. Historical fiction
E. Biography

21.____

22.____

23.____

24.____

25.____

KEY (CORRECT ANSWERS)

1.	C	11.	B
2.	A	12.	D
3.	A	13.	C
4.	D	14.	A
5.	D	15.	D
6.	C	16.	C
7.	B	17.	A
8.	A	18.	B
9.	C	19.	B
10.	B	20.	A

21. E
22. D
23. B
24. C
25. A

EXAMINATION SECTION
TEST 1

DIRECTIONS: Each question or incomplete statement is followed by several suggested answers or completions. Select the one that BEST answers the question or completes the statement. *PRINT THE LETTER OF THE CORRECT ANSWER IN THE SPACE AT THE RIGHT.*

1. Good procedure in handling complaints from the public may be divided into the following four principal stages:
   I. Investigation of the complaint
   II. Receipt of the complaint
   III. Assignment of responsibility for investigation and correction
   IV. Notification of correction

   The ORDER in which these stages ordinarily come is:
   A. III, II, I, IV   B. II, III, I, IV   C. II, III, IV, I   D. II, IV, III, I

2. The department may expect the MOST severe public criticism if
   A. it asks for an increase in its annual budget
   B. it purchases new and costly street cleaning equipment
   C. sanitation officers and men are reclassified to higher salary grades
   D. there is delay in cleaning streets of snow

3. The MOST important function of public relations in the department should be to
   A. develop cooperation on the part of the public in keeping streets clean
   B. get stricter penalties enacted for health code violations
   C. recruit candidates for entrance positions who ca be developed into supervisors
   D. train career personnel so that they can advance in the department

4. The one of the following which has MOST frequently elicited unfavorable public comment has been
   A. dirty sidewalks or streets   B. dumping on lot
   C. failure to curb dogs   D. overflowing garbage cans

5. It has been suggested that, as a public relations measure, sections hold *open house* for the public.
   The MOST effective time for this would be
   A. during the summer when children are not in school and can accompany their parents
   B. during the winter when show is likely to fall and the public can see snow removal preparations
   C. immediately after a heavy snow storm when department snow removal operations are in full progress
   D. when street sanitation is receiving general attention as during *Keep City Clean* week

6. When a public agency conducts a public relations program, it is MOST likely to find that each recipient of its message will
   A. disagree with the basic purpose of the message if the officials are not well known to him
   B. accept the message if it is presented by someone perceived as having a definite intention to persuade
   C. ignore the message unless it is presented in a literate and clever manner
   D. give greater attention to certain portions of the message as a result of his individual and cultural differences

7. Following are three statements about public relations and communications:
   I. A person who seeks to influence public opinion can speed up a trend
   II. Mass communications is the exposure of a mass audience to an idea
   III. All media are equally effective in reaching opinion leaders
   Which of the following choices CORRECTLY classifies the above statements into those which are correct and those which are not?
   A. I and II are correct, but III is not.
   B. II and III are correct, but I is not.
   C. I and III are correct, but II is not.
   D. III is correct, but I and II are not.

8. Public relations experts say that MAXIMUM effect for a message results from
   A. concentrating in one medium
   B. ignoring mass media and concentrating on *opinion makers*
   C. presenting only those factors which support a given position
   D. using a combination of two or more of the available media

9. To assure credibility and avoid hostility, the public relations man MUST
   A. make certain his message is truthful, not evasive or exaggerated
   B. make sure his message contains some dire consequence if ignored
   C. repeat the message often enough so that it cannot be ignored
   D. try to reach as many people and groups as possible

10. The public relations man MUST be prepared to assume that members of his audience
    A. may have developed attitudes toward his proposals—favorable, neutral, or unfavorable
    B. will be immediately hostile
    C. will consider his proposals with an open mind
    D. will invariably need an introduction to his subject

11. The one of the following statements that is CORRECT is:
    A. When a stupid question is asked of you by the public, it should be disregarded
    B. If you insist on formality between you and the public, the public will not be able to ask stupid questions that cannot be answered
    C. The public should be treated courteously, regardless of how stupid their questions may be
    D. You should explain to the public how stupid their questions are

12. With regard to public relations, the MOST important item which should be   12.____
    emphasized in an employee training program is that
    A. each inspector is a public relations agent
    B an inspector should give the public all the information it asks for
    C. it is better to make mistakes and give erroneous information than to tell
       the public that you do not know the correct answer to their problem
    D. public relations is so specialized a field that only persons specially trained
       in it should consider it

13. Members of the public frequently ask about departmental procedures.   13.____
    Of the following, it is BEST to
    A. advise the public to put the question in writing so that he can get a proper
       formal reply
    B. refuse to answer because this is a confidential matter
    C. explain the procedure as briefly as possible
    D. attempt to avoid the issue by discussing other matters

14. The effectiveness of a public relations program in a public agency such as the   14.____
    authority is BEST indicated by the
    A. amount of mass media publicity favorable to the policies of the authority
    B. morale of those employees who directly serve the patrons of the authority
    C. public's understanding and support of the authority's program and policies
    D. number of complaint received by the authority from patrons using its facilities

15. In an attempt to improve public opinion about a certain idea, the BEST course   15.____
    of action for an agency to take would be to present the
    A. clearest statements of the idea even though the language is somewhat
       technical
    B. idea as the result of long-term studies
    C. idea in association with something familiar to most people
    D. idea as the viewpoint of the majority leaders

16. The fundamental factor in any agency's community relations program is   16.____
    A. an outline of the objectives
    B. relations with the media
    C. the everyday actions of the employees
    D. a well-planned supervisory program

17. The FUNDAMENTAL factor in the success of a community relations program is   17.____
    A. true commitment by the community
    B. true commitment by the administration
    C. a well-planned, systematic approach
    D. the actions of individuals in their contacts with the public

18. The statement below which is LEAST correct is:
    A. Because of selection standards, the supervisor frequently encounters problems resulting from subordinates' inability to express themselves in the language of the profession.
    B. Distortion of the meaning of a communication is usually brought about by a failure to use language that has a precise meaning to others.
    C. The term *filtering* is the distortion or dilution of content of a communication that occurs as information is passed from individual to individual.
    D. The complexity of the *communications net* will directly affect.

19. Consider the following three statements that may or may not be CORRECT:
    I. In order to prevent the stifling of communications flow, supervisors should insist that employees use the formal communications network.
    II. Two-way communications are faster and more accurate than one-way communications.
    III. There is a direct correlation between the effectiveness of communications and the total setting in which they occur.
    The choice below which MOST accurately describes the above statement is:
    A. All three are correct.
    B. All three are incorrect.
    C. More than one statement is correct.
    D. Only one of the statements is correct.

20. The statement below which is MOST inaccurate is:
    A. The supervisor's most important tool in learning whether or not he is communicating well is feedback.
    B. Follow-up is essential if useful feedback is to be obtained.
    C. Subordinates are entitled, as a matter of right, to explanations from management concerning the reasons for orders or directives.
    D. A skilled supervisor is often able to use the grapevine to good advantage.

21. *Since concurrence by those affected is not sought, this kind of communication can be issued with relative ease.*
    The kind of communication being referred to in this quotation is
    A. autocratic   B. democratic   C. directive   D. free-rein

22. The statement below which is LEAST correct is:
    A. Clarity is more important in oral communicating than in written since the readers of a written communication can read it over again.
    B. Excessive use of abbreviations in written communications should be avoided.
    C. Short sentences with simple words are preferred over complex sentences and difficult words in a written communication.
    D. The *newspaper* style of writing ordinarily simplifies expression and facilitates understanding.

23. Which one of the following is the MOST important factor for the department to consider in building a good public image?
    A. A good working relationship with the news media
    B. An efficient community relations program
    C. An efficient system for handling citizen complaints
    D. The proper maintenance of facilities and equipment
    E. The behavior of individuals in their contacts with the public.

24. It has been said that the ability to communicate clearly and concisely is the MOST important single skill of the supervisor.
    Consider the following statements:
    I.   The adage, *Actions speak louder than words*, has NO application in superior/subordinate communications since good communications are accomplished with words.
    II. The environment in which a communication takes place will *rarely* determine its effect.
    III. Words are symbolic representations which must be associated with past experience or else they are meaningless.
    The choice below which MOST accurately describes the above statements is:
    A. I, II, and III are correct.
    B. I and II are correct, but III is not.
    C. I and III are correct, but II is not.
    D. III is correct, but I and II are not.
    E. I, II, and III are incorrect.

25. According to expert opinion, the effectiveness of an organization is very dependent upon good upward, downward, and lateral communications. Lateral communications are most important to the activity of coordinating the efforts of organizational units. Before real communication can take place at any level, barriers to communication must be recognized, understood, and removed.
    Consider the following three statements:
    I.   The *principal* barrier to good communications is a failure to establish empathy between sender and receiver.
    II. The difference in status or rank between the sender and receiver of a communication may be a communications barrier.
    III. Communications are easier if they travel upward from subordinate to superior
    The choice below which MOST accurately describes the above statements is:
    A. I, II and III are incorrect.   B. I and II are incorrect.
    C. I, II, and III are correct.   D. I and II are correct.
    E. I and III are incorrect.

KEY (CORRECT ANSWERS)

1.	B		11.	C
2.	D		12.	A
3.	A		13.	C
4.	A		14.	C
5.	D		15.	C
6.	D		16.	C
7.	A		17.	D
8.	D		18.	A
9.	A		19.	D
10.	A		20.	C

21. A
22. A
23. E
24. D
25. E

RECORD KEEPING
EXAMINATION SECTION
TEST 1

DIRECTIONS: Each question or incomplete statement is followed by several suggested answers or completions. Select the one that BEST answers the question or completes the statement. *PRINT THE LETTER OF THE CORRECT ANSWER IN THE SPACE AT THE RIGHT.*

Questions 1-7.

DIRECTIONS: In answering Questions 1 through 7, use the following master list. For each question, determine where the name would fit on the master list. Each answer choice indicates right before or after the name in the answer choice.

    Aaron, Jane
    Armstead, Brendan
    Bailey, Charles
    Dent, Ricardo
    Grant, Mark
    Mars, Justin
    Methieu, Justine
    Parker, Cathy
    Sampson, Suzy
    Thomas, Heather

1. Schmidt, William
   A. Right before Cathy Parker
   B. Right after Heather Thomas
   C. Right after Suzy Sampson
   D. Right before Ricardo Dent

2. Asanti, Kendall
   A. Right before Jane Aaron
   B. Right after Charles Bailey
   C. Right before Justine Methieu
   D. Right after Brendan Armstead

3. O'Brien, Daniel
   A. Right after Justine Methieu
   B. Right before Jane Aaron
   C. Right after Mark Grant
   D. Right before Suzy Sampson

4. Marrow, Alison
   A. Right before Cathy Parker
   B. Right before Justin Mars
   C. Right before Mark Grant
   D. Right after Heather Thomas

5. Grantt, Marissa
   A. Right before Mark Grant
   B. Right after Mark Grant
   C. Right after Justin Mars
   D. Right before Suzy Sampson

1.____

2.____

3.____

4.____

5.____

59

6. Thompson, Heath   6.____
    A. Right after Justin Mars   B. Right before Suzy Sampson
    C. Right after Heather Thomas   D. Right before Cathy Parker

DIRECTIONS: Before answering Question 7, add in all of the names from Questions 1 through 6. Then fit the name in alphabetical order based on the new list.

7. Francisco, Mildred   7.____
    A. Right before Mark Grant   B. Right after Marissa Grantt
    C. Right before Alison Marrow   D. Right after Kendall Asanti

Questions 8-10.

DIRECTIONS: In answering Questions 8 through 10, compare each pair of names and addresses. Indicate whether they are the same or different in any way.

8. William H. Pratt, J.D.   William H. Pratt, J.D.   8.____
    Attourney at Law   Attorney at Law
    A. No differences   B. 1 difference
    C. 2 differences   D. 3 differences

9. 1303 Theater Drive,; Apt. 3-B   1330 Theatre Drive,; Apt. 3-B   9.____
    A. No differences   B. 1 difference
    C. 2 differences   D. 3 differences

10. Petersdorff, Briana and Mary   Petersdorff, Briana and Mary   10.____
     A. No differences   B. 1 difference
     C. 2 differences   D. 3 differences

11. Which of the following words, if any, are misspelled?   11.____
     A. Affordable   B. Circumstansial
     C. Legalese   D. None of the above

Questions 12-13.

DIRECTIONS: Questions 12 and 13 are to be answered on the basis of the following table.

Standardized Test Results for High School Students in District #1230

	English	Math	Science	Reading
High School 1	21	22	15	18
High School 2	12	16	13	15
High School 3	16	18	21	17
High School 4	19	14	15	16

The scores for each high school in the district were averaged out and listed for each subject tested. Scores of 0-10 are significantly below College Readiness Standards. 11-15 are below College Readiness, 16-20 meet College Readiness, and 21-25 are above College Readiness.

12. If the high schools need to meet or exceed in at least half the categories in order to NOT be considered "at risk," which schools are considered "at risk"?   12.____
    A. High School 2   B. High School 3
    C. High School 4   D. Both A and C

13. What percentage of subjects did the district as a whole meet or exceed College Readiness standards?   13.____
    A. 25%   B. 50%   C. 75%   D. 100%

Questions 14-15.

DIRECTIONS: Questions 14 and 15 are to be answered on the basis of the following information.

You have seven employees working as a part of your team: Austin, Emily, Jeremy, Christina, Martin, Harriet, and Steve. You have just sent an e-mail informing them that there will be a mandatory training session next week. To ensure that work still gets done, you are offering the training twice during the week: once on Tuesday and also on Thursday. This way half the employees will still be working while the other half attend the training. The only other issue is that Jeremy doesn't work on Tuesdays and Harriet doesn't work on Thursdays due to compressed work schedules.

14. Which of the following is a possible attendance roster for the first training session?   14.____
    A. Emily, Jeremy, Steve   B. Steve, Christina, Harriet
    C. Harriet, Jeremy, Austin   D. Steve, Martin, Jeremy

15. If Harriet, Christina, and Steve attend the training session on Tuesday, which of the following is a possible roster for Thursday's training session?   15.____
    A. Jeremy, Emily, and Austin   B. Emily, Martin, and Harriet
    C. Austin, Christina, and Emily D. Jeremy, Emily, and Steve

Questions 16-20.

DIRECTIONS: In answering Questions 16 through 20, you will be given a word and will need to choose the answer choice that is MOST similar or different to the word.

16. Which word means the SAME as *annual*?   16.____
    A. Monthly   B. Usually   C. Yearly   D. Constantly

17. Which word means the SAME as *effort*?   17.____
    A. Energy   B. Equate   C. Cherish   D. Commence

18. Which word means the OPPOSITE of *forlorn*?   18.____
    A. Neglected   B. Lethargy   C. Optimistic   D. Astonished

19. Which word means the SAME as *risk*?   19.____
    A. Admire   B. Hazard   C. Limit   D. Hesitant

20. Which word means the OPPOSITE of *translucent*?
    A. Opaque   B. Transparent   C. Luminous   D. Introverted

21. Last year, Jamie's annual salary was $50,000. Her boss called her today to inform her that she would receive a 20% raise for the upcoming year. How much more money will Jamie receive next year?
    A. $60,000   B. $10,000   C. $1,000   D. $51,000

22. You and a co-worker work for a temp hiring agency as part of their office staff. You both are given 6 days off per month. How many days off are you and your co-worker given in a year?
    A. 24   B. 72   C. 144   D. 48

23. If Margot makes $34,000 per year and she works 40 hours per week for all 52 weeks, what is her hourly rate?
    A. $16.34/hour   B. $17.00/hour   C. $15.54/hour   D. $13.23/hour

24. How many dimes are there in $175.00?
    A. 175   B. 1,750   C. 3,500   D. 17,500

25. If Janey is three times as old as Emily, and Emily is 3, how old is Janey?
    A. 6   B. 9   C. 12   D. 15

KEY (CORRECT ANSWERS)

1.	C		11.	B
2.	D		12.	A
3.	A		13.	D
4.	B		14.	B
5.	B		15.	A
6.	C		16.	C
7.	A		17.	A
8.	B		18.	C
9.	C		19.	B
10.	A		20.	A

21.	B
22.	C
23.	A
24.	B
25.	B

TEST 2

DIRECTIONS: Each question or incomplete statement is followed by several suggested answers or completions. Select the one that BEST answers the question or completes the statement. *PRINT THE LETTER OF THE CORRECT ANSWER IN THE SPACE AT THE RIGHT.*

Questions 1-6.

DIRECTIONS: Questions 1 through 6 are to be answered on the basis of the following information.

item	name of item to be ordered
quantity	minimum number that can be ordered
beginning amount	amount in stock at start of month
amount received	amount receiving during month
ending amount	amount in stock at end of month
amount used	amount used during month
amount to order	will need at least as much of each item as used in the previous month
unit price	cost of each unit of an item
total price	total price for the order

Item	Quantity	Beginning	Received	Ending	Amount Used	Amount to Order	Unit Price	Total Price
Pens	10	22	10	8	24	20	$0.11	$2.20
Spiral notebooks	8	30	13	12			$0.25	
Binder clips	2 boxes	3 boxes	1 box	1 box			$1.79	
Sticky notes	3 packs	12 packs	4 packs	2 packs			$1.29	
Dry erase markers	1 pack (dozen)	34 markers	8 markers	40 markers			$16.49	
Ink cartridges (printer)	1 cartridge	3 cartridges	1 cartridge	2 cartridges			$79.99	
Folders	10 folders	25 folders	15 folders	10 folders			$1.08	

1. How many packs of sticky notes were used during the month? 1.____
   A. 16   B. 10   C. 12   D. 14

2. How many folders need to be ordered for next month? 2.____
   A. 15   B. 20   C. 30   D. 40

3. What is the total price of notebooks that you will need to order? 3.____
   A. $6.00   B. $0.25   C. $4.50   D. $2.75

4. Which of the following will you spend the second most money on? 4.____
   A. Ink cartridges   B. Dry erase markers
   C. Sticky notes   D. Binder clips

5. How many packs of dry erase markers should you order? 5.____
   A. 1   B. 8   C. 12   D. 0

6. What will be the total price of the file folders you order?   6._____
   A. $20.16   B. $21.60   C. $10.80   D. $4.32

Questions 7-11.

DIRECTIONS: Questions 7 through 11 are to be answered on the basis of the following table.

| Number of Car Accidents, By Location and Cause, for 2014 |||||||
| | Location 1 || Location 2 || Location 3 ||
Cause	Number	Percent	Number	Percent	Number	Percent
Severe Weather	10		25		30	
Excessive Speeding	20	40	5		10	
Impaired Driving	15		15	25	8	
Miscellaneous	5		15		2	4
TOTALS	50	100	60	100	50	100

7. Which of the following is the third highest cause of accidents for all three locations?   7._____
   A. Severe Weather
   B. Impaired Driving
   C. Miscellaneous
   D. Excessive Speeding

8. The average number of Severe Weather accidents per week at Location 3 for the year (52 weeks) was MOST NEARLY   8._____
   A. 0.57   B. 30   C. 1   D. 1.25

9. Which location had the LARGEST percentage of accidents caused by Impaired Driving?   9._____
   A. 1   B. 2   C. 3   D. Both A and B

10. If one-third of the accidents at all three locations resulted in at least one fatality, what is the LEAST amount of deaths caused by accidents last year?   10._____
    A. 60   B. 106   C. 66   D. 53

11. What is the percentage of accidents caused by miscellaneous means from all three locations in 2014?   11._____
    A. 5%   B. 10%   C. 13%   D. 25%

12. How many pairs of the following groups of letters are exactly alike?   12._____
    ACDOBJ   ACDBOJ
    HEWBWR   HEWRWB
    DEERVS   DEERVS
    BRFQSX   BRFQSX
    WEYRVB   WEYRVB
    SPQRZA   SQRPZA

    A. 2   B. 3   C. 4   D. 5

Questions 13-19.

DIRECTIONS: Questions 13 through 19 are to be answered on the basis of the following information.

In 2012, the most current information on the American population was finished. The information was compiled by 200 volunteers in each of the 50 states. The territory of Puerto Rico, a sovereign of the United States, had 25 people assigned to compile data. In February of 2010, volunteers in each state and sovereign began collecting information. In Puerto Rico, data collection finished by January 31st, 2011, while work in the United States was completed on June 30, 2012. Each volunteer gathered data on the population of their state or sovereign. When the information was compiled, volunteers sent reports to the nation's capital, Washington, D.C. Each volunteer worked 20 hours per month and put together 10 reports per month. After the data was compiled in total, 50 people reviewed the data and worked from January 2012 to December 2012.

13. How many reports were generated from February 2010 to April 2010 in Illinois and Ohio?
    A. 3,000   B. 6,000   C. 12,000   D. 15,000

14. How many volunteers in total collected population data in January 2012?
    A. 10,000   B. 2,000   C. 225   D. 200

15. How many reports were put together in May 2012?
    A. 2,000   B. 50,000   C. 100,000   D. 100,250

16. How many hours did the Puerto Rican volunteers work in the fall (September-November)?
    A. 60   B. 500   C. 1,500   D. 0

17. How many workers were compiling or reviewing data in July 2012?
    A. 25   B. 50   C. 200   D. 250

18. What was the total amount of hours worked by Nevada volunteers in July 2010?
    A. 500   B. 4,000   C. 4,500   D. 5,000

19. How many reviewers worked in January 2013?
    A. 75   B. 50   C. 0   D. 25

20. John has to file 10 documents per shelf. How many documents would it take for John to fill 40 shelves?
    A. 40   B. 400   C. 4,500   D. 5,000

21. Jill wants to travel from New York City to Los Angeles by bike, which is approximately 2,772 miles. How many miles per day would Jill need to average if she wanted to complete the trip in 4 weeks?
    A. 100   B. 89   C. 99   D. 94

22. If there are 24 CPU's and only 7 monitors, how many more monitors do you need to have the same amount of monitors as CPU's?   22._____
    A. Not enough information   B. 17
    C. 31   D. 0

23. If Gerry works 5 days a week and 8 hours each day, and John works 3 days a week and 10 hours each day, how many more hours per year will Gerry work than John?   23._____
    A. They work the same amount of hours.
    B. 450
    C. 520
    D. 832

24. Jimmy gets transferred to a new office. The new office has 25 employees, but only 16 are there due to a blizzard. How many coworkers was Jimmy able to meet on his first day?   24._____
    A. 16   B. 25   C. 9   D. 7

25. If you do a fundraiser for charities in your area and raise $500 total, how much would you give to each charity if you were donating equal amounts to 3 of them?   25._____
    A. $250.00   B. $167.77   C. $50.00   D. $111.11

KEY (CORRECT ANSWERS)

1.	D		11.	C
2.	B		12.	B
3.	A		13.	C
4.	C		14.	A
5.	D		15.	C
6.	B		16.	C
7.	D		17.	B
8.	A		18.	B
9.	A		19.	C
10.	D		20.	B

21.	C
22.	B
23.	C
24.	A
25.	B

TEST 3

DIRECTIONS: Each question or incomplete statement is followed by several suggested answers or completions. Select the one that BEST answers the question or completes the statement. *PRINT THE LETTER OF THE CORRECT ANSWER IN THE SPACE AT THE RIGHT.*

Questions 1-3.

DIRECTIONS: In answering Questions 1 through 3, choose the correctly spelled word.

1. A. allusion B. alusion C. allusien D. allution   1.____
2. A. altitude B. alltitude C. atlitude D. altlitude   2.____
3. A. althogh B. allthough C. althrough D. although   3.____

Questions 4-9.

DIRECTIONS: In answering Questions 4 through 9, choose the answer that BEST completes the analogy.

4. Odometer is to mileage as compass is to   4.____
   A. speed   B. needle   C. hiking   D. direction

5. Marathon is to race as hibernation is to   5.____
   A. winter   B. dream   C. sleep   D. bear

6. Cup is to coffee as bowl is to   6.____
   A. dish   B. spoon   C. food   D. soup

7. Flow is to river as stagnant is to   7.____
   A. pool   B. rain   C. stream   D. canal

8. Paw is to cat as hoof is to   8.____
   A. lamb   B. horse   C. lion   D. elephant

9. Architect is to building as sculptor is to   9.____
   A. museum   B. chisel   C. stone   D. statue

Questions 10-14.

DIRECTIONS: Questions 10 through 14 are to be answered on the basis of the following graph.

Population of Carroll City Broken Down by Age and Gender (in Thousands)			
Age	Female	Male	Total
Under 15	60	60	120
15-23		22	
24-33		20	44
34-43	13	18	31
44-53	20		67
64 and Over	65	65	130
TOTAL	230	232	462

10. How many people in the city are between the ages of 15-23?
    A. 70   B. 46,000   C. 70,000   D. 225,000

11. Approximately what percentage of the total population of the city was female aged 24-33?
    A. 10%   B. 5%   C. 15%   D. 25%

12. If 33% of the males have a job and 55% of females don't have a job, which of the following statements is TRUE?
    A. Males have approximately 2,600 more jobs than females.
    B. Females have approximately 49,000 more jobs than males.
    C. Females have approximately 26,000 more jobs than males.
    D. None of the above statements are true.

13. How many females between the ages of 15-23 live in Carroll City?
    A. 67,000   B. 24,000   C. 48,000   D. 91,000

14. Assume all males 44-53 living in Carroll City are employed. If two-thirds of males age 44-53 work jobs outside of Carroll City, how many work within city limits?
    A. 31,333
    B. 15,667
    C. 47,000
    D. Cannot answer the question with the information provided

Questions 15-16.

DIRECTIONS: Questions 15 and 16 are labeled as shown. Alphabetize them for filing. Choose the answer that correctly shows the order.

15. (1) AED
    (2) OOS
    (3) FOA
    (4) DOM
    (5) COB

    A. 2-5-4-3-2 B. 1-4-5-2-3 C. 1-5-4-2-3 D. 1-5-4-3-2

15.____

16. Alphabetize the names of the people. Last names are given last.
    (1) Lindsey Jamestown
    (2) Jane Alberta
    (3) Ally Jamestown
    (4) Allison Johnston
    (5) Lyle Moreno

    A. 2-1-3-4-5 B. 3-4-2-1-5 C. 2-3-1-4-5 D. 4-3-2-1-5

16.____

17. Which of the following words is misspelled?
    A. disgust   B. whisper
    C. locale   D. none of the above

17.____

Questions 18-21.

DIRECTIONS: Questions 18 through 21 are to be answered on the basis of the following list of employees.

    Robertson, Aaron
    Bacon, Gina
    Jerimiah, Trace
    Gillette, Stanley
    Jacks, Sharon

18. Which employee name would come in third in alphabetized list?
    A. Robertson, Aaron   B. Jerimiah, Trace
    C. Gillette, Stanley   D. Jacks, Sharon

18.____

19. Which employee's first name starts with the letter in the alphabet that is five letters after the first letter of their last name?
    A. Jerimiah, Trace   B. Bacon, Gina
    C. Jacks, Sharon   D. Gillette, Stanley

19.____

20. How many employees have last names that are exactly five letters long?
    A. 1   B. 2   C. 3   D. 4

20.____

21. How many of the employees have either a first or last name that starts with the letter "G"?   21.____
    A. 1   B. 2   C. 4   D. 5

Questions 22-25.

DIRECTIONS: Questions 22 through 25 are to be answered on the basis of the following chart.

Bicycle Sales (Model #34JA32)							
Country	May	June	July	August	September	October	Total
Germany	34	47	45	54	56	60	296
Britain	40	44	36	47	47	46	260
Ireland	37	32	32	32	34	33	200
Portugal	14	14	14	16	17	14	89
Italy	29	29	28	31	29	31	177
Belgium	22	24	24	26	25	23	144
Total	176	198	179	206	208	207	1166

22. What percentage of the overall total was sold to the German importer?   22.____
    A. 25.3%   B. 22%   C. 24.1%   D. 23%

23. What percentage of the overall total was sold in September?   23.____
    A. 24.1%   B. 25.6%   C. 17.9%   D. 24.6%

24. What is the average number of units per month imported into Belgium over the first four months shown?   24.____
    A. 26   B. 20   C. 24   D. 31

25. If you look at the three smallest importers, what is their total import percentage?   25.____
    A. 35.1%   B. 37.1%   C. 40%   D. 28%

KEY (CORRECT ANSWERS)

1.	A		11.	B
2.	A		12.	C
3.	D		13.	C
4.	D		14.	B
5.	C		15.	D
6.	D		16.	C
7.	A		17.	D
8.	B		18.	D
9.	D		19.	B
10.	C		20.	B

21.	B
22.	A
23.	C
24.	C
25.	A

TEST 4

DIRECTIONS: Each question or incomplete statement is followed by several suggested answers or completions. Select the one that BEST answers the question or completes the statement. *PRINT THE LETTER OF THE CORRECT ANSWER IN THE SPACE AT THE RIGHT.*

Questions 1-6.

DIRECTIONS: In answering Questions 1 through 6, choose the sentence that represents the BEST example of English grammar.

1. A. Joey and me want to go on a vacation next week. 1.____
   B. Gary told Jim he would need to take some time off.
   C. If turning six years old, Jim's uncle would teach Spanish to him.
   D. Fax a copy of your resume to Ms. Perez and me.

2. A. Jerry stood in line for almost two hours. 2.____
   B. The reaction to my engagement was less exciting than I thought it would be.
   C. Carlos and me have done great work on this project.
   D. Two parts of the speech needs to be revised before tomorrow.

3. A. Arriving home, the alarm was tripped. 3.____
   B. Jonny is regarded as a stand up guy, a responsible parent, and he doesn't give up until a task is finished.
   C. Each employee must submit a drug test each month.
   D. One of the documents was incinerated in the explosion.

4. A. As soon as my parents get home, I told them I finished all of my chores. 4.____
   B. I asked my teacher to send me my missing work, check my absences, and how did I do on my test.
   C. Matt attempted to keep it concealed from Jenny and me.
   D. If Mary or him cannot get work done on time, I will have to split them up.

5. A. Driving to work, the traffic report warned him of an accident on Highway 47. 5.____
   B. Jimmy has performed well this season.
   C. Since finishing her degree, several job offers have been given to Cam.
   D. Our boss is creating unstable conditions for we employees.

6. A. The thief was described as a tall man with a wiry mustache weighing approximately 150 pounds. 6.____
   B. She gave Patrick and I some more time to finish our work.
   C. One of the books that he ordered was damaged in shipping.
   D. While talking on the rotary phone, the car Jim was driving skidded off the road.

2 (#4)

Questions 7-9.

DIRECTIONS: Questions 7 through 9 are to be answered on the basis of the following graph.

Ice Lake Frozen Flight (2002-2013)		
Year	Number of Participants	Temperature (Fahrenheit)
2002	22	4°
2003	50	33°
2004	69	18°
2005	104	22°
2006	108	24°
2007	288	33°
2008	173	9°
2009	598	39°
2010	698	26°
2011	696	30°
2012	777	28°
2013	578	32°

7. Which two year span had the LARGEST difference between temperatures?   7.____
   A. 2002 and 2003   B. 2011 and 2012
   C. 2008 and 2009   D. 2003 and 2004

8. How many total people participated in the years after the temperature   8.____
   reached at least 29°?
   A. 2,295   B. 1,717   C. 2,210   D. 4,543

9. In 2007, the event saw 288 participants, while in 2008 that number   9.____
   dropped to 173. Which of the following reasons BEST explains the drop in
   participants?
      A. The event had not been going on that long and people didn't know about it.
      B. The lake water wasn't cold enough to have people jump in.
      C. The temperature was too cold for many people who would have normally participated.
      D. None of the above reasons explain the drop in participants.

10. In the following list of numbers, how many times does 4 come just after 2   10.____
    when 2 comes just after an odd number?
    2365247653898632488572486392424
    A. 2   B. 3   C. 4   D. 5

11. Which choice below lists the letter that is as far after B as S is after N in   11.____
    the alphabet?
    A. G   B. H   C. I   D. J

Questions 12-15.

DIRECTIONS: Questions 12 through 15 are to be answered on the basis of the following directory and list of changes.

Directory		
Name	Emp. Type	Position
Julie Taylor	Warehouse	Packer
James King	Office	Administrative Assistant
John Williams	Office	Salesperson
Ray Moore	Warehouse	Maintenance
Kathleen Byrne	Warehouse	Supervisor
Amy Jones	Office	Salesperson
Paul Jonas	Office	Salesperson
Lisa Wong	Warehouse	Loader
Eugene Lee	Office	Accountant
Bruce Lavine	Office	Manager
Adam Gates	Warehouse	Packer
Will Suter	Warehouse	Packer
Gary Lorper	Office	Accountant
Jon Adams	Office	Salesperson
Susannah Harper	Office	Salesperson

Directory Updates:
- Employee e-mail addresses will adhere to the following guidelines: lastnamefirstname@apexindustries.com (ex. Susannah Harper is harpersusannah@apexindustries.com). Currently, employees in the warehouse share one e-mail, distribution@apexindustries.com.
- The "Loader" position will now be referred to as "Specialist I"
- Adam Gates has accepted a Supervisor position within the Warehouse and is no longer a Packer. All warehouse employees report to the two Supervisors and all office employees report to the Manager.

12. Amy Jones tried to send an e-mail to Adam Gates, but it wouldn't send. Which of the following offers the BEST explanation?
    A. Amy put Adam's first name first and then his last name.
    B. Adam doesn't check his e-mail, so he wouldn't know if he received the e-mail or not.
    C. Adam does not have his own e-mail.
    D. Office employees are not allowed to send e-mails to each other.

13. How many Packers currently work for Apex Industries?
    A. 2   B. 3   C. 4   D. 5

14. What position does Lisa Wong currently hold?
    A. Specialist I   B. Secretary
    C. Administrative Assistant   D. Loader

15. If an employee wanted to contact the office manager, which of the following e-mails should the e-mail be sent to?
    A. officemanager@apexindustries.com
    B. brucelavine@apexindustries.com
    C. lavinebruce@apexindustries.com
    D. distribution@apexindustries.com

15.____

Questions 16-19.

DIRECTIONS: In answering Questions 16 through 19, compare the three names, numbers or addresses.

16. Smiley Yarnell   Smiley Yarnel   Smily Yarnell   16.____
    A. All three are exactly alike.
    B. The first and second are exactly alike.
    C. The second and third are exactly alike.
    D. All three are different.

17. 1583 Theater Drive   1583 Theater Drive   1583 Theatre Drive   17.____
    A. All three are exactly alike.
    B. The first and second are exactly alike.
    C. The second and third are exactly alike.
    D. All three are different.

18. 3341893212   3341893212   3341893212   18.____
    A. All three are exactly alike.
    B. The first and second are exactly alike.
    C. The second and third are exactly alike.
    D. All three are different.

19. Douglass Watkins   Douglas Watkins   Douglass Watkins   19.____
    A. All three are exactly alike.
    B. The first and third are exactly alike.
    C. The second and third are exactly alike.
    D. All three are different.

Questions 20-24.

DIRECTIONS: In answering Questions 20 through 24, you will be presented with a word. Choose the synonym that BEST represents the word in question.

20. Flexible   20.____
    A. delicate   B. inflammable   C. strong   D. pliable

21. Alternative   21.____
    A. choice   B. moderate   C. lazy   D. value

22. Corroborate
    A. examine   B. explain   C. verify   D. explain   22.____

23. Respiration
    A. recovery   B. breathing   C. sweating   D. selfish   23.____

24. Negligent
    A. lazy   B. moderate   C. hopeless   D. lax   24.____

25. Plumber is to Wrench as Painter is to   25.____
    A. pipe   B. shop   C. hammer   D. brush

KEY (CORRECT ANSWERS)

1. D
2. A
3. D
4. C
5. B

6. C
7. C
8. B
9. C
10. C

11. A
12. C
13. A
14. A
15. C

16. D
17. B
18. A
19. B
20. D

21. A
22. C
23. B
24. D
25. D

EXAMINATION SECTION
TEST 1

DIRECTIONS: Each question or incomplete statement is followed by several suggested answers or completions. Select the one that BEST answers the question or completes the statement. *PRINT THE LETTER OF THE CORRECT ANSWER IN THE SPACE AT THE RIGHT.*

Questions 1-5.

DIRECTIONS: Questions 1 through 5 consist of a sentence with an underlined word. For each question, select the choice that is CLOSEST in meaning to the underlined word.

EXAMPLE
This division reviews the fiscal reports of the agency.
In this sentence, the word *fiscal* means MOST NEARLY
   A. financial   B. critical   C. basic   D. personnel
The correct answer is A. "financial" because "financial" is closest to *fiscal*. Therefore, the answer is A.

1. Every good office worker needs basic skills.   1.____
   The word *basic* in this sentence means
      A. fundamental   B. advanced   C. unusual   D. outstanding

2. He turned out to be a good instructor.   2.____
   The word *instructor* in this sentence means
      A. student   B. worker   C. typist   D. teacher

3. The quantity of work in the office was under study.   3.____
   In this sentence, the word *quantity* means
      A. amount   B. flow   C. supervision   D. type

4. The morning was spent examining the time records.   4.____
   In this sentence, the word *examining* means
      A. distributing   B. collecting   C. checking   D. filing

5. The candidate filled in the proper spaces on the form.   5.____
   In this sentence, the word *proper* means
      A. blank   B. appropriate   C. many   D. remaining

Questions 6-8.

DIRECTIONS: Questions 6 through 8 are to be answered SOLELY on the basis of the information contained in the following paragraph.

The increase in the number of public documents in the last two centuries closely matches the increase in population in the United States. The great number of public documents has become a serious threat to their usefulness. It is necessary to have programs which will reduce the number of public documents that are kept and which will, at the same time, assure keeping those that have value. Such programs need a great deal of thought to have any success.

6. According to the above paragraph, public documents may be less useful if 6.____
   A. the files are open to the public
   B. the record room is too small
   C. the copying machine is operated only during normal working hours
   D. too many records are being kept

7. According to the above paragraph, the growth of the population in the United 7.____
   States has matched the growth in the quantity of public documents for a period
   of MOST NEARLY _____ years.
   A. 50   B. 100   C. 200   D. 300

8. According to the above paragraph, the increased number of public documents 8.____
   has made it necessary to
   A. find out which public documents are worth keeping
   B. reduce the great number of public documents by decreasing government services
   C. eliminate the copying of all original public documents
   D. avoid all new copying devices

Questions 9-10.

DIRECTIONS: Questions 9 and 10 are to be answered SOLELY on the basis of the information contained in the following paragraph.

The work goals of an agency can best be reached if the employees understand and agree with these goals. One way to gain such understanding and agreement is for management to encourage and seriously consider suggestions from employees in the setting of agency goals.

9. On the basis of the above paragraph, the BEST way to achieve the work goals 9.____
   of an agency is to
   A. make certain that employees work as hard as possible
   B. study the organizational structure of the agency
   C. encourage employees to think seriously about the agency's problems
   D. stimulate employee understanding of the work goals

10. On the basis of the above paragraph, understanding and agreement with agency   10.____
goals can be gained by
   A. allowing the employees to set agency goals
   B. reaching agency goals quickly
   C. legislative review of agency operations
   D. employee participation in setting agency goals

Questions 11-15.

DIRECTIONS: Each of Questions 11 through 15 consists of a group of four words. One word in each group is incorrectly spelled. For each question, print the letter of the correct answer in the space at the right that is the same as the letter next to the word which is INCORRECTLY spelled.

EXAMPLE

   A. housing   B. certain   C. budgit   D. money

The word "budgit" is incorrectly spelled, because the correct spelling should be "budget." Therefore, the correct answer is C.

11.   A. sentince   B. bulletin   C. notice   D. definition   11.____

12.   A. appointment   B. exactly   C. typest   D. light   12.____

13.   A. penalty   B. suparvise   C. consider   D. division   13.____

14.   A. schedule   B. accurate   C. corect   D. simple   14.____

15.   A. suggestion   B. installed   C. proper   D. agincy   15.____

Questions 16-20.

DIRECTIONS: Each Question 16 through 20 consists of a sentence which may be
   A. incorrect because of bad word usage, or
   B. incorrect because of bad punctuation, or
   C. incorrect because of bad spelling, or
   D. correct
Read each sentence carefully. Then print in the space at the right A, B, C, or D, according to the answer you choose from the four choices listed above. There is only one type of error in each incorrect sentence. If there is no error, the sentence is correct.

EXAMPLE

George Washington was the father of his contry.
This sentence is incorrect because of bad spelling ("contry" instead of "country").
Therefore, the answer is C.

4 (#1)

16. The assignment was completed in record time but the payroll for it has not yet been preparid.

16.____

17. The operator, on the other hand, is willing to learn me how to use the mimeograph.

17.____

18. She is the prettiest of the three sisters.

18.____

19. She doesn't know; if the mail has arrived.

19.____

20. The doorknob of the office door is broke.

20.____

21. A clerk can process a form in 15 minutes.
    How many forms can that clerk process in six hours?
       A. 10   B. 21   C. 24   D. 90

21.____

22. An office staff consists of 120 people. Sixty of them have been assigned to a special project. Of the remaining staff, 20 answer the mail, 10 handle phone calls, and the rest operate the office machines.
    The number of people operating the office machines is
       A. 20   B. 30   C. 40   D. 45

22.____

23. An office worker received 65 applications but on the first day had to return 26 of them for being incomplete and on the second day 25 had to be returned for being incomplete.
    How many applications did NOT have to be returned?
       A. 10   B. 12   C. 14   D. 16

23.____

24. An office worker answered 63 phone calls in one day and 91 phone calls the next day.
    For these 2 days, what was the average number of phone calls he answered per day?
       A. 77   B. 28   C. 82   D. 93

24.____

25. An office worker processed 12 vouchers of $8.50 each, 3 vouchers of $3.68 each, and 2 vouchers of $1.29 each.
    The TOTAL dollar amount of these vouchers is
       A. $116.04   B. $117.52   C. $118.62   D. $119.04

25.____

KEY (CORRECT ANSWERS)

1.	A	11.	A
2.	D	12.	C
3.	A	13.	B
4.	C	14.	C
5.	B	15.	D
6.	D	16.	C
7.	C	17.	A
8.	A	18.	D
9.	D	19.	B
10.	D	20.	A

21. C
22. B
23. C
24. A
25. C

TEST 2

DIRECTIONS: Each question or incomplete statement is followed by several suggested answers or completions. Select the one that BEST answers the question or completes the statement. *PRINT THE LETTER OF THE CORRECT ANSWER IN THE SPACE AT THE RIGHT.*

Questions 1-5.

DIRECTIONS: Each Question from 1 through 5 lists four names. The names may not be exactly the same. Compare the names in each question and mark your answer
    A if all the names are different
    B if only two names are exactly the same
    C if only three names are exactly the same
    D if all four names are exactly the same

EXAMPLE
Jensen, Alfred E.
Jensen, Alfred E.
Jensan, Alfred E.
Jensen, Fred E.

Since the name Jensen, Alfred E. appears twice and is exactly the same in both places, the correct answer is B.

1.   A. Riviera, Pedro S.   B. Rivers, Pedro S.   1.____
    C. Riviera, Pedro N.   D. Riviera, Juan S.

2.   A. Guider, Albert   B. Guidar, Albert   2.____
    C. Giuder, Alfred   D. Guider, Albert

3.   A. Blum, Rona   B. Blum, Rona   3.____
    C. Blum, Rona   D. Blum, Rona

4.   A. Raugh, John   B. Raugh, James   4.____
    C. Raughe, John   D. Raugh, John

5.   A. Katz, Stanley   B. Katz, Stanley   5.____
    C. Katze, Stanley   D. Katz, Stanley

Questions 6-10.

DIRECTIONS: Each Question 6 through 10 consists of numbers or letters in Columns I and II. For each question, compare each line of Column I with its corresponding line in Column II and decide how many lines in Column I are EXACTLY the same as their corresponding lines in Column II. In your answer space, mark your answer
    A if only ONE line in Column I is exactly the same as its corresponding line in Column II
    B if only TWO lines in Column I are exactly the same as their corresponding lines in Column II

2 (#2)

    C if only THREE lines in Column I are exactly the same as their corresponding lines in Column II
    D if all FOUR lines in Column I are exactly the same as their corresponding lines in Column II

EXAMPLE

Column I	Column II
1776	1776
1865	1865
1945	1945
1976	1978

Only three lines in Column I are exactly the same as their corresponding lines in Column II. Therefore, the correct answer is C.

	Column I	Column II	
6.	5653 8727 ZPSS 4952	5653 8728 ZPSS 9453	6.____
7.	PNJP NJPJ JNPN PNJP	PNPJ NJPJ JNPN PNPJ	7.____
8.	effe uWvw KpGj vmnv	eFfe uWvw KpGg vmnv	8.____
9.	5232 PfrC zssz rwwr	5232 PfrN zzss rwww	9.____
10.	czws cecc thrm lwtz	czws cece thrm lwtz	10.____

Questions 11-15.

DIRECTIONS: Questions 11 through 15 have lines of letters and numbers. Each letter should be matched with its number in accordance with the following table.

Letter	F	R	C	A	W	L	E	N	B	T
Matching Number	0	1	2	3	4	5	6	7	8	9

From the table you can determine that the letter F has the matching number 0 below it, the letter R has the matching number 1 below, etc.

For each question, compare each line of letters and numbers carefully to see if each letter has its correct matching number. If all the letters and numbers are matched correctly in

    none of the lines of the question, mark your answer A
    only *one* of the lines of the question, mark your answer B
    only *two* of the lines of the question, mark your answer C
    all three lines of the question, mark your answer D

EXAMPLE

WBCR	4826
TLBF	9580
ATNE	3986

There is a mistake in the first line because the letter R should have its matching number 1 instead of the number 6.

The second line is correct because each letter shown has the correct matching number.

There is a mistake in the third line because the letter N should have the matching number 7 instead of the number 8.

Since all the letters and numbers are correct matched in only one of the lines in the sample, the correct answer is B.

11.   EBCT   6829   11._____
       ATWR   3961
       NLBW   7584

12.   RNCT   1729   12._____
       LNCR   5728
       WAEB   5368

13.   NTWB   7948   13._____
       RABL   1385
       TAEF   9360

14.   LWRB   5417   14._____
       RLWN   1647
       CBWA   2843

15.   ABTC   3792   15._____
       WCER   5261
       AWCN   3417

16. Your job often brings you into contact with the public.   16._____
Of the following, it would be MOST desirable to explain the reasons for official actions to people coming into your office for assistance because such explanations
     A. help build greater understanding between the public and your agency
     B. help build greater self-confidence in city employees
     C. convince the public that nothing they do can upset a city employee
     D. show the public that city employees are intelligent

17. Assume that you strongly dislike one of your co-workers.
    You should FIRST
    A. discuss your feeling with the co-worker
    B. demand a transfer to another office
    C. suggest to your supervisor that the co-worker should be observed carefully
    D. try to figure out the reason for this dislike before you say or do anything

18. An office worker who has problems accepting authority is MOST likely to find it difficult to
    A. obey rules
    B. understand people
    C. assist other employees
    D. follow complex instructions

19. The employees in your office have taken a dislike to one person and frequently annoy her.
    Your supervisor should
    A. transfer this person to another unit at the first opportunity
    B. try to find out the reason for the staff's attitude before doing anything about it
    C. threaten to transfer the first person observed bothering this person
    D. ignore the situation

20. Assume that your supervisor has asked a worker in your office to get a copy of a report out of the files. You notice the worker as accidentally pulled out the wrong report.
    Of the following, the BEST way for you to handle this situation is to tell
    A. the worker about all the difficulties that will result from this error
    B. the worker about her mistake in a nice way
    C. the worker to ignore this error
    D. your supervisor that this worker needs more training in how to use the files

21. Filing systems differ in their efficiency.
    Which of the following is the BEST way to evaluate the efficiency of a filing system? A
    A. number of times used per day
    B. amount of material that is received each day for filing
    C. amount of time it takes to locate material
    D. type of locking system used

22. In planning ahead so that a sufficient amount of general office supplies is always available, it would be LEAST important to find out the
    A. current office supply needs of the staff
    B. amount of office supplies used last year
    C. days and times that office supplies can be ordered
    D. agency goals and objectives

5 (#2)

23. The MAIN reason for establishing routine office work procedures is that once a routine is established
    A. work need not be checked for accuracy
    B. all steps in the routine will take an equal amount of time to perform
    C. each time the job is repeated, it will take less time to perform
    D. each step in the routine will not have to be planned all over again each time

24. When an office machine centrally located in an agency must be shut down for repairs, the bureaus and divisions using this machine should be informed of the
    A. expected length of time before the machine will be in operation again
    B. estimated cost of repairs
    C. efforts being made to avoid future repairs
    D. type of new equipment which the agency may buy in the future to replace the machine being repaired

25. If the day's work is properly scheduled, the MOST important result would be that the
    A. supervisor will not have to do much supervision
    B. employee will know what to do next
    C. employee will show greater initiative
    D. job will become routine

KEY (CORRECT ANSWERS)

1.	A		11.	C
2.	B		12.	B
3.	D		13.	D
4.	B		14.	B
5.	C		15.	A
6.	B		16.	A
7.	B		17.	D
8.	B		18.	A
9.	A		19.	B
10.	C		20.	B

21. C
22. D
23. D
24. A
25. B

NAME AND NUMBER CHECKING
EXAMINATION SECTION
TEST 1

DIRECTIONS: This test is designed to measure your speed/and accuracy. You are urged to work both quickly and accurately and to do correctly as many lists as you can in the time allowed. The test consists of lists or pairs of names and numbers. Count the number of IDENTICAL pairs in each list. Then, select the correct number, 1, 2, 3, 4, 5, and indicate your choice in the space at the right. Two sample questions are presented for your guidance, together with the correct solutions.

SAMPLE LIST A
Adelphi College – Adelphia College
Braxton Corp – Braxeton Corp.
Wassaic State School – Wassaic State School
Central Islip State Hospital – Central Isllip State Hospital
Greenwich House – Greenwich House

NOTE: There are only two correct pairs—Wassaic State School and Greenwich House. Therefore, the CORRECT answer is 2.

SAMPLE LIST B
78453694 – 78453684
784530 – 784530
533 – 534
67845 – 67845
2368745 – 2368755

NOTE: There are only two correct pairs—784530 and 67845. Therefore, the CORRECT answer is 2.

LIST 1   1.____
    Diagnostic Clinic   – Diagnostic Clinic
    Yorkville Health   – Yorkville Health
    Meinhard Clinic   – Meinhart Clinic
    Corlears Clinic   – Carlears Clinic
    Tremont Diagnostic   – Tremont Diagnostic

LIST 2   2.____
    73526   – 73526
    7283627198   – 7283627198
    627   – 637
    728352617283   – 7283526178282
    6281   – 6281

2 (#1)

LIST 3   3.____
    Jefferson Clinic   – Jeffersen Clinic
    Mott Haven Center   – Mott Havan Center
    Bronx Hospital   – Bronx Hospital
    Montefiore Hospital   – Montifeore Hospital
    Beth Isreal Hospital   – Beth Israel Hospital

LIST 4   4.____
    936271826   – 936371826
    5271   – 5291
    82637192037   – 82637192037
    527182   – 5271882
    726354256   - 72635456

LIST 5   5.____
    Trinity Hospital   – Trinity Hospital
    Central Harlem   – Centrel Harlem
    St. Luke's Hospital   – St. Lukes' Hospital
    Mt. Sinai Hospital   – Mt. Sinia Hospital
    N.Y. Dispensery   – N.Y. Dispensary

LIST 6   6.____
    725361552637   – 725361555637
    7526378   – 7526377
    6975   – 6975
    82637481028   – 82637481028
    3427   – 3429

LIST 7   7.____
    Misericordia Hospital   – Miseracordia Hospital
    Lebonan Hospital   – Lebanon Hospital
    Gouverneur Hospital   – Gouverner Hospital
    German Polyclinic   – German Policlinic
    French Hospital   – French Hospital

LIST 8   8.____
    8277364933251   – 827364933351
    63728   – 63728
    367281   – 367281
    62733846273   – 6273846293
    62836   - 6283

LIST 9   9.____
    King's County Hospital   – Kings County Hospital
    St. Johns Long Island   – St. John's Long Island
    Bellevue Hospital   – Bellvue Hospital
    Beth David Hospital   – Beth David Hospital
    Samaritan Hospital   – Samariton Hospital

3 (#1)

LIST 10
    62836454   – 62836455
    42738267   – 42738369
    573829   – 573829
    738291627874   – 738291627874
    725   - 735

10.____

LIST 11
    Bloomingdal Clinic   – Bloomingdale Clinic
    Communitty Hospital   – Community Hospital
    Metroplitan Hospital   – Metropoliton Hospital
    Lenox Hill Hospital   – Lonex Hill Hospital
    Lincoln Hospital   – Lincoln Hospital

11.____

LIST 12
    6283364728   – 6283648
    627385   – 627383
    54283902   – 54283602
    63354   – 63354
    7283562781   - 7283562781

12.____

LIST 13
    Sydenham Hospital   – Sydanham Hospital
    Roosevalt Hospital   – Roosevelt Hospital
    Vanderbilt Clinic   – Vanderbild Clinic
    Women's Hospital   – Woman's Hospital
    Flushing Hospital   – Flushing Hospital

13.____

LIST 14
    62738   – 62738
    727355542321   – 72735542321
    263849332   – 263849332
    262837   – 263837
    47382912   - 47382922

14.____

LIST 15
    Episcopal Hospital   – Episcapal Hospital
    Flower Hospital   – Flouer Hospital
    Stuyvesent Clinic   – Stuyvesant Clinic
    Jamaica Clinic   – Jamaica Clinic
    Ridgwood Clinic   – Ridgewood Clinic

15.____

LIST 16
    628367299   – 628367399
    111   – 111
    118293304829   – 1182839489
    4448   – 4448
    333693678   - 333693678

16.____

4 (#1)

LIST 17   17.____
    Arietta Crane Farm   – Areitta Crane Farm
    Bikur Chilim Home   – Bikur Chilom Home
    Burke Foundation   – Burke Foundation
    Blythedale Home   – Blythdale Home
    Campbell Cottages   – Cambell Cottages

LIST 18   18.____
    32123   – 32132
    273893326783   – 27389326783
    473829   – 473829
    7382937   – 7383937
    3628890122332   - 36289012332

LIST 19   19.____
    Caraline Rest   – Caroline Rest
    Loreto Rest   – Loretto Rest
    Edgewater Creche   – Edgwater Creche
    Holiday Farm   – Holiday Farm
    House of St. Giles   – House of st. Giles

LIST 20   20.____
    557286777   – 55728677
    3678902   – 3678892
    1567839   – 1567839
    7865434712   – 7865344712
    9927382   - 9927382

LIST 21   21.____
    Isabella Home   – Isabela Home
    James A. Moore Home   – James A. More Home
    The Robin's Nest   – The Roben's Nest
    Pelham Home   – Pelam Home
    St. Eleanora's Home   – St. Eleanora's Home

LIST 22   22.____
    273648293048   – 273648293048
    334   – 334
    7362536478   – 7362536478
    7362819273   – 7362819273
    7362   - 7363

LIST 23   23.____
    St. Pheobe's Mission   – St. Phebe's Mission
    Seaside Home   – Seaside Home
    Speedwell Society   – Speedwell Society
    Valeria Home   – Valera Home
    Wiltwyck   - Wildwyck

5 (#1)

LIST 24 | | 24.____
:--- | :--- |
63728 | – 63738
63728192736 | – 63728192738
428 | – 458
62738291527 | – 62738291529
63728192 | - 63728192

LIST 25 | | 25.____
:--- | :--- |
McGaffin | – McGafin
David Ardslee | – David Ardslee
Axton Supply | – Axeton Supply Co
Alice Russell | – Alice Russell
Dobson Mfg. Co. | – Dobsen Mfg. Co.

KEY (CORRECT ANSWERS)

1.	3		11.	1
2.	3		12.	2
3.	1		13.	1
4.	1		14.	2
5.	1		15.	1
6.	2		16.	3
7.	1		17.	1
8.	2		18.	1
9.	1		19.	1
10.	2		20.	2

21.	1
22.	4
23.	2
24.	1
25.	2

TEST 2

DIRECTIONS: This test is designed to measure your speed/and accuracy. You are urged to work both quickly and accurately and to do correctly as many lists as you can in the time allowed. The test consists of lists or pairs of names and numbers. Count the number of IDENTICAL pairs in each list. Then, select the correct number, 1, 2, 3, 4, 5, and indicate your choice in the space at the right.

LIST 1   1.____
    82637381028   – 82637281028
    928   – 928
    72937281028   – 72937281028
    7362   – 7362
    927382615   – 927382615

LIST 2   2.____
    Albee Theatre   – Albee Theatre
    Lapland Lumber Co.   – Laplund Lumber Co.
    Adelphi College   – Adelphi College
    Jones & Son Inc.   – Jones & Sons Inc.
    S.W. Ponds Co.   – S.W. Ponds Co.

LIST 3   3.____
    85345   – 85345
    895643278   – 895643277
    726352   – 726353
    632685   – 632685
    7263524   – 7236524

LIST 4   4.____
    Eagle Library   – Eagle Library
    Dodge Ltd.   – Dodge Co.
    Stromberg Carlson   – Stromberg Carlsen
    Clairice Ling   – Clairice Linng
    Mason Book Co.   – Matson Book Co.

LIST 5   5.____
    66273   – 66273
    629   – 629
    7382517283   – 7382517283
    637281   – 639281
    2738261   – 2788261

LIST 6   6.____
    Robert MacColl   – Robert McColl
    Buick Motor   – Buck Motors
    Murray Bay & Co. Ltd. – Murray Bay Co. Ltd.
    L.T. Ltyle   – L.T. Lyttle
    A.S. Landas   – A.S. Landas

LIST 7
 6271526374890   – 627152637490
 73526189   – 73526189
 5372   – 5392
 637281142   – 63728124
 4783946   – 4783046

7.____

LIST 8
 Tyndall Burke   – Tyndell Burke
 W. Briehl   – W. Briehl
 Burritt Publishing Co.   – Buritt Publishing Co.
 Frederick Breyer & Co.   – Frederick Breyer Co.
 Bailey Buulard   – Bailey Bullard

8.____

LIST 9
 634   – 634
 16837   – 163837
 273892223678   – 27389223678
 527182   – 527782
 3628901223   – 3629002223

9.____

LIST 10
 Ernest Boas   – Ernest Boas
 Rankin Barne   – Rankin Barnes
 Edward Appley   – Edward Appely
 Camel   – Camel
 Caiger Food Co.   – Caiger Food Co.

10.____

LIST 11
 6273   – 6273
 322   – 332
 15672839   – 15672839
 63728192637   – 63728192639
 738   – 738

11.____

LIST 12
 Wells Fargo Co.   – Wells Fargo Co.
 W.D. Brett   – W.D. Britt
 Tassco Co.   – Tassko Co.
 Republic Mills   – Republic Mill
 R.W. Burnham   – R.W. Burhnam

12.____

LIST 13
 7253529152   – 7283529152
 6283   – 6383
 52839102738   – 5283910238
 308   – 398
 82637201927   – 8263720127

13.____

3 (#2)

LIST 14   14.____
    Schumacker Co.   – Shumacker Co.
    C.H. Caiger   – C.H. Caiger
    Abraham Strauss   – Abram Straus
    B.F. Boettjer   – B.F. Boettijer
    Cut-Rate Store   – Cut-Rate Stores

LIST 15   15.____
    15273826   – 15273826
    72537   – 73537
    726391027384   – 62639107384
    637389   – 627399
    725382910   – 725382910

LIST 16   16.____
    Hixby Ltd.   – Hixby Lt'd.
    S. Reiner   – S. Riener
    Reynard Co.   – Reynord Co.
    Esso Gassoline Co.   – Esso Gasolene Co.
    Belle Brock   – Belle Brock

LIST 17   17.____
    7245   – 7245
    819263728192   – 819263728172
    682537289   – 682537298
    789   – 789
    82936542891   – 82936542891

LIST 18   18.____
    Joseph Cartwright   – Joseph Cartwrite
    Foote Food Co.   – Foot Food Co.
    Weiman & Held   – Weiman & Held
    Sanderson Shoe Co.   – Sandersen Shoe Co.
    A.M. Byrne   – A.N. Byrne

LIST 19   19.____
    4738267   – 4738277
    63728   – 63729
    6283628901   – 6283628991
    918264   – 918264
    263728192037   – 2637728192073

LIST 20   20.____
    Exray Laboratories   – Exray Labratories
    Curley Toy Co.   – Curly Toy Co.
    J. Lauer & Cross   – J. Laeur & Cross
    Mireco Brands   – Mireco Brands
    Sandor Lorand   – Sandor Larand

4 (#2)

LIST 21   21.____
    607   – 609
    6405   – 6403
    976   – 996
    101267   – 101267
    2065432   – 20965432

LIST 22   22.____
    John Macy & Sons   – John Macy & Son
    Venus Pencil Co.   – Venus Pencil Co.
    Nell McGinnis   – Nell McGinnis
    McCutcheon & Co.   – McCutcheon & Co.
    Sun-Tan Oil   – Sun-Tan Oil

LIST 23   23.____
    703345700   – 703345700
    46754   – 466754
    3367490   – 3367490
    3379   – 3778
    47384   – 47394

LIST 24   24.____
    arthritis   – arthritis
    asthma   – asthma
    endocrine   – endocrene
    gastro-enterological   – gastrol-enteralogical
    orthopedic   – orthopedic

LIST 25   25.____
    743829432   – 743828432
    998   – 998
    732816253902   – 732816252902
    46829   – 46830
    7439120249   – 7439210249

KEY (CORRECT ANSWERS)

1.	4		11.	3
2.	3		12.	1
3.	2		13.	1
4.	1		14.	1
5.	2		15.	2
6.	1		16.	1
7.	2		17.	3
8.	1		18.	1
9.	1		19.	1
10.	3		20.	1

21. 1
22. 4
23. 2
24. 3
25. 1

LIBRARY SCIENCE

TABLE OF CONTENTS

	Page
LIBARIES AND LIBRARIANSHIP	1
BACKGROUND	1
Introduction	1
History of Libraries	1
Growth of Libraries in the United States	1
Professionalization	2
FACETS AND SCOPE OF LIBRARIANSHIP	2
Demand for Libraries in the Economy	2
Public Libraries	2
School Libraries	2
College and University Libraries	3
Special Libraries	3
The Modern Library	3
OCCUPATIONAL DESCRIPTIONS	4
Acquisitions Librarian	4
Bookmobile Driver	4
Bookmobile Librarian	4
Cataloger	5
Chief Librarian	5
Children's Librarian	6
Classifier	6
Collector, Overdue Material	7
Field Librarian	7
Film Librarian	8
Librarian	8
Librarian, Special Collections	9
Librarian, Special Library	9
Library Assistant	10
Library Associate Director	10
Library Director	11
Page	11
Patients' Librarian	11
Registration Clerk	12
School Librarian	12
Shelving Supervisor	12
Young Adult Librarian	13

LIBRARY SCIENCE

LIBRARIES AND LIBRARIANSHIP

BACKGROUND

INTRODUCTION
In the history of man, the communication of ideas has been the factor which distinguishes him from the lower animals. The ability to pass on knowledge and culture through the medium of speech led to the growth of civilization. Just as important, however, was the development of a means of preserving knowledge through written records, for it is this accumulated wealth of information which has enabled man to control his environment and to uncover some of the mysteries of the earth and heavens.

Throughout recorded history, it has been the duty of the librarian to preserve and organize the books and other records which contain man's knowledge and ideas so that they may be used most effectively to further the growth of civilization.

HISTORY OF LIBRARIES
Libraries have existed ever since man has written. Ancient Egypt boasted collections of papyrus rolls, while the Babylonians and Assyrians gathered together their cuneiform covered clay tablets so that they could be cataloged and preserved. Undoubtedly, the two most famous libraries of the ancient world were at Alexandria. In the third century B.C., only a few years after their founding, the larger of the two was reported to contain over a half million papyrus rolls. Some of the earliest experiments in bibliography were the catalogs of the Alexandrian libraries.

It was in ancient Rome that public libraries flourished in abundance and that the science of librarianship became recognized. The first large book collections were acquired as the spoils of war. The Romans realized their importance and enlarged them, in addition to building library collections of their own. In the fourth century, Rome had twenty-eight public libraries. With the fall of the Empire, however, books were withdrawn to monasteries and private collections. Not until the advent of the printing press in the middle of the fifteenth century did books again become plentiful and libraries again grow.

GROWTH OF LIBRARIES IN THE UNITED STATES
There have been books and libraries in the United States since the early days of the Colonies. The first organized library was founded in 1638 at Harvard University. As other colleges were instituted in the Colonies, they too established libraries for the use of their faculties and students. Public libraries did not come as quickly. The nearest approach to public library service was the subscription library, the first being Benjamin Franklin's Library Company, organized in Philadelphia in 1731 The first public library in the United States to be directly established by state legislation was the Boston library. In1838, Massachusetts passed legislation specifically designed to allow the city of Boston to establish a public library and to appropriate municipal funds for its support. Earlier, Peterborough, New Hampshire, formed the first tax-supported library in 1833 on the basis of a state law passed in 1821 permitting a certain portion of tax revenue to be used for schools and other educational purposes

PROFESSIONALIZATION

The years between 1850 and 1870 saw a period of rapid growth. Not only were college and public libraries flourishing, but governmental and specialized libraries achieved importance; and as the prestige of libraries grew, so did the role of the librarian and his responsibility. Librarianship became a profession in its own right. Realizing that librarians needed an organization to help them to utilize more fully the available materials and to standardize procedures, Melvil Dewey and other prominent members of the profession called a nationwide meeting of librarians in 1876, and the American Library Association was founded. This was the first of many professional organizations which have arisen to meet the needs of librarians in the ever-widening fields of knowledge which they serve.

FACETS AND SCOPE OF LIBRARIANSHIP

DEMAND FOR LIBRARIANS IN THE ECONOMY

As the scope of man's knowledge has increased and as the numbers of his written works have grown, so have libraries and the need for librarians. At the first meeting of the American Library Association in 1876, only one hundred and four persons were present. At that time, there were approximately 1,000 librarians in the United States. It was estimated that there were more than 150,000 active professional librarians. Public libraries, colleges, and universities, schools, governmental agencies, public and private institutions, and commercial and industrial firms all have need of the librarian's services.

In general, it may be said that librarianship is a service profession, one in which the individual, no matter what his level of responsibility or specialization, devotes his time to satisfying the needs of others to obtain informational material. Because so many of the agencies, firms, and institutions cited above have realized the importance of having trained librarians administer to the needs of their staffs, faculties, students, or patrons, the demand for librarians continues to increase. According to the United States Department of Labor, the number of librarians is expected to increase by 4.9%, while library technicians increase by 13.4% and library assistants by 12.5% by 2014.

While the largest number of 2000 graduates (32%) were placed in college and university libraries, the need for librarians in many phases of activity can be seen from the fact that 29% of the graduates accepted positions in public libraries, 21% became school librarians, and 18% undertook special and other library work.

PUBLIC LIBRARIES

The public library in the United States today is a tax-supported institution, providing direct service to all members of the community. Informational, educational, and recreational materials are available, with special programs for work with children and young people, older persons, and adult education groups. The librarians involved in these programs must be knowledgeable as to the books and other materials available and the particular psychology of the age and social groups of the people whom they are serving.

SCHOOL LIBRARIES

The school library is established by the educational governing body, usually the Board of Education, in a school community to provide books and other educational materials to the children and faculties in the elementary and secondary schools. The librarian in a school library is usually required to have a background in educational theories as well as a degree in Library Science since he or she must provide supplementary teaching aids.

COLLEGE AND UNIVERSITY LIBRARIES

The college or university library, like the school library, is established to serve the particular community of an educational institution. Research materials are stressed. In the large universities, there may be several libraries, each one serving an individual college or department, i.e., the science library, medical school library, or art school library.

SPECIAL LIBRARIES

The field of special librarianship is widely diversified. In general, there are two types of special libraries: (1) The special organization library, serving all informational needs of an organization such as a corporation or governmental agency, in which both the staff and clientele are employees of the same organization; (2) the special subject library, which may be semi-public, independent, departmental, or branch library, serving students, professional groups, or members on a given subject. The special librarian must often be a specialist in a particular field of information. He must be aware of current publications and research, and be able to assemble, organize, and maintain this information so that it may be of greatest use to the library's clientele.

THE MODERN LIBRARY

The modern library, recognizing the many media of communication available today, includes a variety of materials in its collection. Not only are books and periodicals found on library shelves, but many institutions provide audio/video material, advanced media and internet access to patrons, along with the records, films, and slides that remain vital even in today's advanced technological age. A few public libraries have framed paintings and other pictures which may be borrowed. Braille and talking books for the blind are available, as are ceiling-protected books for the bedridden.

Modern methods are used to increase library efficiency. Microfilm and digital copies of magazines and newspapers are important space-savers, as well as effective means of preserving information. Various systems of photographic charging of materials have resulted in a saving of man-hours and an elimination of many errors.

One of the newest ways in which libraries are utilizing modern science is in the use of automatic data processing systems for library cataloging and documentation. The introduction of these new systems has been brought about by the fact that in the second half of the 20th century and into the new millennium, the production of information has accelerated with startling speed and intensity. Approximately 50% of all scholarly material available today has been produced in the last fifteen years; there are now approximately 50,000 technical journals being published, and the number is expected to increase at the rate of 1,000 yearly; in scientific areas, it has been estimated that up to 2 million articles are published yearly.

New theories are being developed and new techniques are being applied to handle this flow of information. Complex electronic and mechanical means of information storage and retrieval are being developed to organize, catalog, classify, and index the wide diversity of information.

It is in the special library, the research library, and in specialized areas of the public library where the greatest concentration of information control has taken place. A number of organizations have created large information exchange networks, spanning the continent. In the future, it is expected that countries around the world will participate in the operation of information exchange systems.

OCCUPATIONAL DESCRIPTIONS

ACQUISITIONS LIBRARIAN
0-23.10
(100.288)

OCCUPATIONAL DEFINITION

Selects and orders books, periodicals, films, and other materials for library. Reviews publishers' announcements and catalogs, and compiles lists of publications to be purchased. Compares selections with card catalog and orders-in-process to avoid duplication. Circulates selection list to branches and departments for comments. Selects vendors on basis of such factors as discount allowances and delivery dates. Compiles statistics on purchases, such as total purchases, average price, and fund allocations. May recommend acquisition of materials from individuals or organizations or by exchange with other libraries. Collaborates daily with other units, with additional library staff, and with vendors and publishers to provide optimal access to library materials for the community. Will participate in providing materials budget estimates, establishing fund allocations, monitoring expenditures and fiscal closing.

EDUCATIONAL AND TRAINING REQUIREMENTS
Master's degree in Library Science. Training time, from 1 to 2 years.

BOOKMOBILE DRIVER
7-36.260
(109.368)

OCCUPATIOAL DEFINITION

Drives bookmobile or light truck that pulls book trailer, and assists in providing library services in mobile library. Drives vehicle to specified locations on predetermined schedule. Places books and periodicals on shelves according to such groupings as subject matter, readers' age grouping, or reading level. Stamps dates on library cards, files cards, and collects fines. Compiles reports of mileage, number of books issued, and amount of fines collected. Drives vehicle to garage for repairs, such as motor or transmission overhauls, and for preventive maintenance, such as chassis lubrication and oil change. Charges and discharges library material, in a timely manner. Assists patrons in locating appropriate library materials. Responds to ready reference questions. Takes application and issues library cards.

EDUCATIONAL AND TRAINING REQUIREMENTS
Tenth grade or above. Training time, approximately two months.

BOOKMOBILE LIBRARIAN
0-23.20
(100.168)

OCCUPATIONAL DEFINITION

Provides library services for mobile library within given geographical area: Surveys community needs, and selects books and other materials for library. Publicizes visits to area to stimulate reading interest. May prepare special collections for schools and other groups. May arrange bookmobile schedule. May drive bookmobile. (This job is a specialization of LIBRARIAN and shares the same basic duties.)

EDUCATIONAL AND TRAINING REQUIREMENTS
Master's degree in Library Science. Training time, three months.

CATALOGER
0-23.10
(100.388)
Catalog librarian; descriptive cataloger.

OCCUPATIONAL DEFINITION
 Compiles information on library materials, such as books and periodicals, and prepares catalog cards to identify materials and to integrate information into library catalog: Verifies author, title, and classification number on sample catalog card received from CLASSIFIER against corresponding data on title page. Fills in additional information, such as publisher, date of publication, and edition. Examines material and notes additional information, such as bibliographies, illustrations, maps, and appendices. Copies classification number from sample card into library material for identification. Files card in assigned sections of catalog. Tabulates number of sample cards according to quantity of material and catalog subject headings to determine number of new cards to be ordered or reproduced. Prepares inventory cards to record purchase information and location of library material. Requisitions additional cards. Records new information, such as death date of author and revised edition date, to amend cataloged cards. May specialize in regularly issued publications such as journals, periodicals, and bulletins, and be known as Serials Cataloger. In some instances, depending on the needs of the particular library system, the duties of CATALOGER and CLASSIFIER are combined into one occupation given the title of CATALOGER.

EDUCATIONAL AND TRAINING REQUIREMENTS
Master's degree in Library Science. Training time, one year.

CHIEF LIBRARIAN – BRANCH OR DEPARTMENT
0-23.20
(100.168)

OCCUPATIONAL DEFINITION
 Supervises staff, coordinates activities of library branch or department, and assists patrons in selection and location of books, films, audio/video items, web applications, and other materials. Trains and assigns duties to workers. Directs workers in performance of such tasks as receiving, shelving, and locating materials. Examines book reviews, publishers' catalogs, and other information sources to recommend material acquisition. Supervises and directs the arrangement of materials on shelves or in files according to classification code, titles, or authors' names. Selects materials such as newspaper clippings and pictures to maintain special collections. Searches catalog files, biographical dictionaries, and indexes, and examines content of reference materials to assist patrons in locating and selecting materials. May assemble and arrange materials for display. May

prepare replies to mail requests for information. May compile lists of library materials and recommend materials to individuals or groups and be designated Readers'Advisory-Service Librarian. May be designated according to type of library as Chief Librarian, Branch; Chief Librarian, Bookmobile; or according to department as Chief Librarian, Art Department; Chief Librarian, Circulation Department; Chief Librarian, Music Department; Chief Librarian, Readers' Advisory Service.

EDUCATIONAL AND TRAINING REQUIREMENTS
Master's degree in Library Science. Training time of 2 to 4 years serving in various professional positions in a library system. Experience should reflect proven ability to supervise others.

CHILDREN'S LIBRARIAN
0-23.20
(100.168)

OCCUPATIONAL DEFINITION
Assists children in selecting and locating library materials, and organizes and conducts activities for children to encourage reading and use of library facilities: Confers with teachers, parents, and community groups to relate library services to the concerns of adults working with children. Stimulates children's discriminate reading by organizing such activities as story hours, reading clubs, book fairs, and summer reading programs. Shows films, tell stories, and gives book talks to encourage reading. Conducts library tours to acquaint children with library facilities and services. (This job is a specialization of LIBRARIAN and shares the same basic duties.)

EUCATIONAL AND TRAINING REQUIREMENTS
Master's degree in Library Science. Training time, six months to one year.

CLASSIFIER
0-23.1
(100.388)
Subject cataloger

OCCUPATIONAL DEFINITION
Classifies library materials such as books, films, audio/video material and periodicals according to subject matter: Reviews materials to be classified and searches information sources, such as book reviews, encyclopedias, online reference material and technical publications, to determine subject matter of materials.
Selects classification numbers and descriptive headings according to Dewey Decimal, Library of Congress, or other library classification systems. Makes sample cards containing author, title, and classification number to guide CATALOGER in preparing catalog cards for books and periodicals. Assigns classification numbers, descriptive headings, and explanatory summaries to book and catalog cards to facilitate locating and obtaining materials. Composes annotations (explanatory summaries) of material content.

EDUCATIONAL AND TRAINING REQUIREMENTS
Master's degree in Library Science. Training time, from 1 to 4 years, depending on areas of responsibility, and size and complexity of library system.

COLLECTOR, OVERDUE MATERIAL
1-15.69
(240.368)

OCCUPATIONAL DEFINITION
Collects fines and overdue library material from borrowers: Sorts copies of overdue notices, according to street addresses, to plan collection route. Drives to address shown on overdue notice and explains purpose of call to borrower. Attempts to obtain overdue material and fine, or library card. Collects payment for lost material. Schedules return appointment to obtain material not on premises or advises borrower of alternative methods of returning materials. Records reasons for failure to collect material on overdue notice.

EDUCATIONAL AND TRAINING REQUIREMENTS
High school graduate. Training time, one week.

FIELD LIBRARIAN
0-23.01
(100.118)
Library consultant; state field consultant

OCCUPATIONAL DEFINITION
Advises administrators, members of trustee boards, and civic groups on matters designed to improve the organization, administration, and service of public libraries: Discusses personnel staffing patterns, building plans, and book collections with administrators who request consultation service from State. Analyzes administrative policies, observes work procedures, and reviews data relative to book collections to determine effectiveness of library service to public. Compares allotments designated for building funds, salaries, and book collections with standards prepared by State agencies, to determine effectiveness of budget. Gathers statistical data, such as population and community growth rates, and analyzes building plans to determine adequacy of programs for expansion. Prepares evaluation of library systems based on observations and surveys, and recommends measures to improve organization and administration of systems according to state program for libraries and professional experience. Presents surveys of salary standards, budget analyses, and tentative building programs to administrators as suggested means of improving administration of library systems. Negotiates with civic groups, boards of trustees, and library administrators who wish to consolidate library systems to resolve jurisdictional disputes and differences of opinion. Informs citizen groups of state legal requirements relative to library consolidations. Explains eligibility requirements for programs offering State and Federal financial assistance to libraries and recommends measures to be taken to attain eligibility and apply for aid. Plans and organizes programs for the recruitment of professional personnel. Directs the establishment of work procedures in new or reorganized library systems. Recommends methods of enlarging book collections. Plans and organizes training programs for administrators to inform them of recent developments in public administration and library

science. Addresses town meetings and civic organizations to explain programs offered by State Division of Libraries. Occasionally demonstrates or performs all professional and clerical tasks associated with public libraries.

EDUCATIONAL AND TRAINING REQUIREMENTS
Master's degree in Library Science. Approximately five years of experience in professional library work, with at least two years as administrator.

FILM LIBRARIAN
0-23.10
(100.168)
Audiovisual librarian; film-and-record librarian

OCCUPATIONAL DEFINITION
Plans film programs and keeps library of film and other audio-visual materials: Reviews records/CDs and motion-picture soundtracks, and motion pictures, considering their technical, informational, and esthetic qualities, to select materials for library collection. Prepares brief summary of film content for catalog. Prepares and arranges film programs for presentation to groups. Advises those planning to install film program on technical problems, such as acoustics, lighting, and program content, and leads discussions after film showing. May maintain or oversee maintenance of audio and video material. Operates audio/visual equipment, film projectors, CD/DVD players, splicers, rewinders, and film-inspection equipment.

EDUCATIONAL AND TRAINING REQUIREMENTS
Master's degree in Library Science with additional training in film production techniques.

LIBRARIAN
0-23.20
(100.168)

OCCUPATIONAL DEFINITION
Selects and maintains library collection of books, periodicals, documents, films, recordings, media technology and other materials, and assists groups and individuals to locate and obtain materials: Furnishes information on library activities, facilities, rules, and services. Explains use of reference sources, such as bibliographic indexes, reading guides, the internet and online applications to locate information. Describes or demonstrates procedures for searching catalog files, shelf collections and online and media applications to obtain materials. Searches catalog files and shelves to locate information. Issues and receives materials for circulation or for use in library. Assembles and arranges displays of books and other library materials. Performs variety of duties to maintain reference and circulation matter, such as copying author's name and title on catalog cards, and selecting and assembling pictures and newspaper clippings. Answers correspondence on special reference subjects. May compile book titles, bibliographies, or reading lists according to subject matter or designated interests to prepare reading lists. May select, order, catalog and classify materials. Librarians also compile lists of books, periodicals, articles, and audio-visual materials on particular subjects; analyze collections; and recommend materials. They collect and organize books, pamphlets, manuscripts, and

other materials in a specific field, such as rare books, genealogy, or music. In addition, they coordinate programs such as storytelling for children and literacy skills and book talks for adults, conduct classes, publicize services, provide reference help, write grants, and oversee other administrative matters. When engaged in locating information on specific subjects is known as Reference Librarian.

EDUCATIONAL AND TRAINING REQUIREMENTS
Master's degree in Library Science. Training time of six months to two years, depending on nature of assignment.

LIBRARIAN, SPECIAL COLLECTIONS
0-23.10
(100.168)

OCCUPATIONAL DEFINITION
Collects books, pamphlets, manuscripts, and rare newspapers, to provide source material for research: Organizes collections according to field of interest. Examines reference works and consults specialists preparatory to selecting materials for collections. Compiles bibliographies. Appraises subject materials, using references, such as bibliographies, book auction records, and special catalogs. Publishes papers and bibliographies on special collections to notify clientele of available materials. Lectures on booklore, such as history of printing, bindings, and illuminations. May plan and arrange displays for library exhibits. May index and reproduce materials for sale to other libraries. May specialize in rare books and be known as Rare Book Librarian.

EDUCATIONAL AND TRAINING REQUIREMENTS
Master's degree in Library Science. Training time may range up to five years, depending on complexity of field and size of collection.

LIBRARIAN, SPECIAL LIBRARY
0-23.20
(100.118)

OCCUPATIONAL DEFINITION
Manages library or section containing specialized materials for industrial, commercial, or governmental organizations, or for such institutions as schools and hospitals: Arranges special collections of technical books, periodicals, manufacturers' catalogs and specifications, film strips, motion pictures, CD/DVD and other media, and journal reprints. Searches literature, compiles accession lists, and annotates or abstracts materials. Assists patrons in research problems. May translate or order translation of materials from foreign languages into English. May be designated according to subject matter or specialty of library or department as Art Librarian; Business Librarian; Engineering Librarian; Law Librarian; Map Librarian; Medical Librarian.

EDUCATIONAL AND TRAINING REQUIREMENTS
Master's degree in Library Science. Training time, 1 to 2 years.

LIBRARY ASSISTANT
1-20.01
(100.368)

OCCUPATIONAL DEFINITION

Compiles records, sorts and shelves books, and issues and receives library materials, such as books, films, and CD-ROM: Records identifying data and due date on cards by hand or using photographic equipment to issue books to patrons. Inspects returned books for damage, verifies due date, and computes and receives overdue fines. Reviews records to compile list of overdue books and issues overdue notices to borrowers. Sorts books, publications, and other item according to classification code and returns them to shelves, files, or other designated storage area. Locates books and publications for patrons. Issues borrower's identification card according to established procedures. Files cards in catalog drawers according to system. Repairs books. Answers inquiries of nonprofessional nature on telephone and in person and refers persons requiring professional assistance to LIBRARIAN. May type material cards or issue cards and duty schedules. May be designated according to type of library as Bookmobile Clerk; Branch-Library Clerk; according to assigned department as Library Clerk, Art Department; or may be known according to tasks performed as Library Clerk, Book Return.

EDUCATIONAL AND TRAINING REQUIREMENTS
High school graduate. Training time, 6 to 12 months.

LIBRARY ASSOCIATE DIRECTOR
0-23.01
(100.118)

OCCUPATIONAL DEFINITION

Directs and assists with formulation and administration of library policies and procedures: Confers with department heads to coordinate reference services with technical processing and circulation activities. Meets with subordinate supervisory personnel to discuss goals and problems in library system. Observes functions in branch libraries to insure that established policies and work procedures are followed. Confers with LIBRARY DIRECTOR to discuss methods for increasing the efficiency of library service. Recommends reclassification of library jobs based on specific criteria of job evaluation, such as complexity of duties and scope of responsibility. Visits colleges, universities, and professional organizations to recruit workers. Forecasts growth of community from analysis of statistical data and plans building programs and expansion of library service into new areas. Acts for LIBRARY DIRECTOR in his absence.

EDUCATIONAL AND TRAINING REQUIREMENTS
Master's degree in Library Science. Training time, approximately 4 to 6 years, serving in various professional and supervisory positions in a library system.

LIBRARY DIRECTOR
0-23.01
(100.118)

OCCUPATIONAL DEFINITION
    Plans and administers program of library services: Submits recommendations on library policies and services to governing body, such as board of directors or board of trustees, and implements policy decisions. Analyzes, selects, and executes recommendations of subordinates, such as department chiefs or branch supervisors. Analyzes and coordinates departmental budget estimates and controls expenditures to administer approved budget. Reviews and evaluates orders for books, film, and advanced media, examines trade publications and samples, interviews publishers' representatives, and consults with subordinates to select materials. Administers personnel regulations, interviews and appoints job applicants, rates staff performance, and promotes and discharges employees. Plans and conducts staff meetings and participates in community and professional committee meetings to discuss library problems. Delivers book reviews and lectures to publicize library activities and services. May examine and select materials to be discarded, repaired, or replaced. May be designated according to governmental subdivision served as City-Library Director; County-Library Director.

EDUCATIONAL AND TRAINING REQUIREMENTS
Master's degree in Library Science. Training time, approximately 4 to 8 years, serving in various professional and supervisory positions in a library system.

PAGE
1-23.14
(109.687)
Library page; runner; shelver; shelving clerk; stack clerk.

OCCUPATIONAL DEFINITION
    Locates library materials such as books, periodicals, and pictures for loan, and replaces material in shelving area stacks) or files, according to identification number and title. Trucks or carries material between shelving area and issue desk. May cut premarked articles from periodicals.

EDUCATIONAL AND TRAINING REQUIREMENTS
Tenth to twelfth grade. Training time, from 1 to 3 months.

PATIENTS' LIBRARIAN
0-23.20
(100.168)
Hospital librarian.

OCCUPATIONAL DEFINITION
    Analyzes reading needs of patients and provides library services for patients and employees in hospital or similar institution: Furnishes readers' advisory services on basis of knowledge of current reviews and bibliographies. Reviews requests, and selects books and other library materials for ward trips according to mental state, educational

background, and special needs of patients. Writes book reviews for hospital bulletins or newspapers and circulates reviews among patients. Provides handicapped or bedridden patients with reading aids, such as prism glasses, page turners, book stands, or talking books, and with other audio-visual material and aids. (This job is a specialization of LIBRARIAN and shares the same basic duties. See LIBRARIAN.)

EDUCATIONAL AND TRAINING REQUIREMENTS
Master's degree in Library Science. Training time, six months.

REGISTRATION CLERK
1-20.01
(109.368)

OCCUPATIONAL DEFINITION
Registers library patrons to permit them to borrow books, periodicals, and other library materials: Copies identifying data, such as name and address, from application onto registration list and borrowers' cards to register borrowers, and issues cards to borrowers. Records changes of address or name onto registration list and borrowers' cards to amend records.

EDUCATIONAL AND TRAINING REQUIREMENTS
High school graduate. Training time, 6 to 12 months.

SCHOOL LIBRARIAN
0-23.20
(100.168)

OCCUPATIONAL DEFINITION
Provides library service which includes book and audio-visual material selection, circulation, promotional work, reference, and general administration: Serves as a resource specialist for teachers, counselors, and other faculty members. Guides students in their reading and in use of communication media. (This job is a specialization of LIBRARIAN and shares the same basic duties. See LIBRARIAN.)

EDUCATIONAL AND TRAINING REQUIREMENTS
Master's degree in Library Science. Training time, 6 months to 2 years.

SHELVING SUPERVISOR
1-20.01
(109.138)

OCCUPATIONAL DEFINITION
Supervises and coordinates activities of library workers engaged in replacing books and other materials on shelves according to library classification system: Assigns duties to workers. Trains and directs workers in performance of shelving tasks. Examines materials on shelves to verify accuracy of placement. Counts number of materials placed

on shelves to record shelving activity. Marks designated classification number, subject matter, or title, to arrange material for shelving.

EDUCATIONAL AND TRAINING REQUIREMENTS
High school graduate. Training time, one year.

YOUNG ADULT LIBRARIAN
0-23.10
(100.288)

OCCUPATIONAL DEFINITION
    Directs young adult program in library to provide special activities for high school and college-age readers: Organizes young adults activities, such as chess clubs, creative writing club, and photography contests. Contacts speakers, writers, and distributes advertising, and meets young adult club representatives to prepare group programs. Delivers talks on books to stimulate reading. Addresses groups such as parent-teacher associations and civic organizations, to inform community of activities. Conducts high school classes on Library Tours to acquaint students with library facilities and services. Compiles lists of young adult reading materials for individuals, high school classes, and branch libraries. Issues and receives library materials, such as books and phonograph records. (This job is a specialization of LIBRARIAN and shares the same basic duties. See LIBRARIAN.)

EDUCATIONAL AND TRAINING REQUIREMENTS
Master's degree in Library Science with an additional one year training time.

BASIC FUNDAMENTALS OF LIBRARY SCIENCE

TABLE OF CONTENTS

	Page
DEWEY DECIMAL SYSTEM	1
PREPARING TO USE THE LIBRARY	1
THREE TYPES OF BOOK CARDS	2
Author Card	2
Title Card	2
Subject Card	3
Call Number	3
PERIODICALS	3
PERIODICALS FILE	3
PERIODICAL INDEXES	3
TEST IN LIBRARY SCIENCE	4
I. Using a Card Catalog	4
II. Understanding Entries in a Periodical Index	5
III. Identifying Library Terms	7
IV. Finding a Book by its Call Number	7
V. General	9
KEY (CORRECT ANSWERS)	10

BASIC FUNDAMENTALS OF LIBRARY SCIENCE

The problem of classifying' all human knowledge has produced a branch of learning called "library science." A lasting contribution to a simple and understandable method of locating a book on any topic was designed by Melvil Dewey in 1876. His plan divided all knowledge into ten large classes and then dubdivided each class according to related groups.

DEWEY DECIMAL SYSTEM

1. Subject Classification

The Dewey Decimal Classification System is the accepted and most widely used subject classification system in libraries throughout the world.

2. Classification by Three (3) Groups

There are three groups of classification in the system. A basic group of ten (10) classifications arranges all knowledge as represented by books within groups by classifications numbered 000-900.

The second group is the "100 division"; each group of the basic "10 divisions" is again divided into 9 sub-sctions allowing for more detailed and specialized subjects not identified in the 10 basic divisions.

3. There is a third, still further specialized "One thousand" group where each of the "100" classifications are further divided by decimalized, more specified, subject classifications. The "1,000" group is mainly used by highly specialized scientific and much diversified libraries.

These are the subject classes of the Dewey System:

000-099	General works (included bibliography, encyclopedias, collections, periodicals, newspapers,etc.)
100-199	Philosophy (includes psychology, logic, ethics, conduct, etc.) 200-299 Religion (includes mythology, natural theology, Bible, church history, etc.)
300-399	Social Science (includes economics, government, law, education, commerce, etc.)
400-499	Language (includes dictionaries, grammars, philology, etc.) 500-599 Science (includes mathematics, chemistry, physics, astronomy, geology, etc.) 600-699 Useful Arts (includes agriculture, engineering, aviation, medicine, manufactures, etc.) 700-799 Fine Arts (includes sculpture, painting, music, photography, gardening, etc.)
800-899	Literature (includes poetry, plays, orations, etc.) 900-999 History (includes geoegraphy, travel, biography, ancient and modern history, etc.)

PREPARING TO USE THE LIBRARY

Your ability to use the library and its resources is an important factor in determining your success. Skill and efficiency in finding the library materials you need for assignments and research papers will increase the amount of time you have to devote to reading or organizing information.

These are some of the preparations you can make now.
1. Develop skill in using your local library. You can increase your familiarity with the card catalog and the periodical indexes, such as the *Readers' Guide to Periodical Literature, in* any library.
2. Take the *Test in Library Science* to see how you can improve your knowledge of the library.
3. Read in such books as *Books, Libraries and You* by Jessie Edna Boyd, *The Library Key* by Margaret G. Cook, and *Making Books Work, a Guide to the Use of Libraries* by Jennie Maas Flexner.

You can find other titles by looking under the subject heading LIBRARIES AND READERS in the card catalog of your library. THREE TYPES OF BOOK CARDS

Here are the three general types of cards which are used to represent a book in the main catalog.

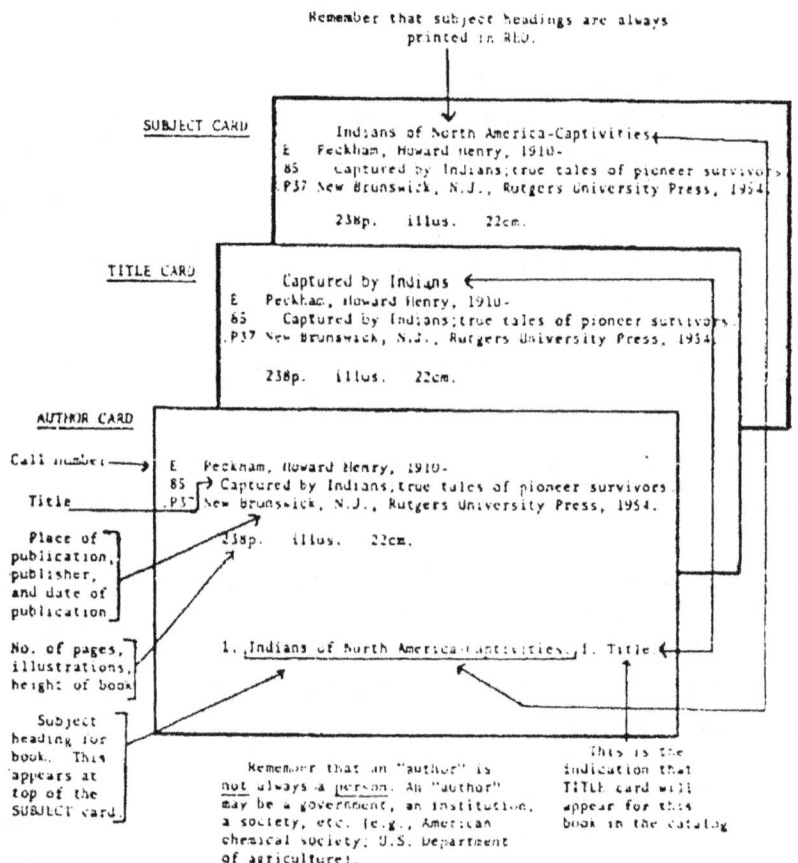

CARD CATALOG

The Card Catalog lists all books in the library by author. The majority of books also have title and subject cards.

Author card

If the author is known, look in the catalog under the author's name. The "author" for some works may be a society, an institution, or a government department.

Title card

Books with distinctive titles, anonymous works and periodicals will have a title card.

Subject card
To find books on a specific subject, look in the catalog under that subject heading. (Subject headings are printed in red on the Catalog Card.)

Call number
The letters and numbers in the upper left-hand corner *of the* Catalog Card are the book's call number. Copy this call number accurately, for it will determine the shelf location of the book. The word "Reference" marked in red in the upper right-hand corner of the catalog card indicates that the item is shelved in the Reference Section,and "Periodical "marked in yellow on the Catalog Card indicates that the item is shelved in the Periodicals Section. PERIODICALS

All magazines are arranged in alphabetical order by title. PERIODICALS FILE

To determine whether the Library has a specific magazine, consult the Periodicals File. Check the title of the magazine needed, and note that there are two cards for each title.

The bottom card lists the current issues available. The top card lists back bound volumes.

Those marked "Ask at Ref.Desk" may be obtained from the Reference Librarian. PERIODICAL INDEXES

Material in magazines is more up-to-date than books and is a valuable source of information. To find articles on a chosen subject, use the periodical indexes.

The Readers' Guide to Periodical Literature is the most familiar of these indexes. In the front of each volume is a list of the periodicals indexed and a key to abbreviations. Similar aids appear in the front of other periodical indexes.

Sample entry: WEASELS

        WONDERFUL WHITE WEASEL. R.Beck. il OUTDOOR LIFE 135:48-9+ Ja '65

Explanation :   An illustrated article on the subject WEASELS entitled WONDERFUL WHITE WEASEL, by R.Beck,will be found in volume 135 of OUTDOOR LIFE, pages 48-9 (continued on later pages of the same issue), the January 1965 number.

Major libraries subscribe to the following indexes:

Art Index
Biography Index
Book Review Index
British Humanities Index
Essay and General Literature Index
    This is helpful for locating criticism of works of literature.
An Index to Book Reviews in the Humanities
International Index ceased publications June, 1965 and continued as Social Science and
     Humanities Index
The Music Index The New York
Times Index Nineteenth Century Readers' Guide
Poole's Index
Poverty and Human Resources Abstracts
Psychological Abstracts
Public Affairs Information Service.Bulletin of the (PAIS) is a subject index to current
     books,pamphlets,periodical articles, government documents, and other library materials in economics and public affairs.

Readers' Guide to Periodical Literature
Social Science and Humanities Index a continuation of the International Index
Sociological Abstracts

Do you have the basic skills for using a library efficiently? You should be able to answer AT LEAST 33 of the following questions correctly. *CHECK YOUR ANSWERS BY TURNING TO THE ANSWER KEY AT THE BACK OF THIS SECTION.*
USING A CARD CATALOG
Questions 1-9.

DIRECTIONS: An author card (or "main entry" card) is shown below. Identify each item on the card by selecting the CORRECT letters for them. *PRINT THE LETTER OF THE CORRECT ANSWER IN THE SPACE AT THE RIGHT.*

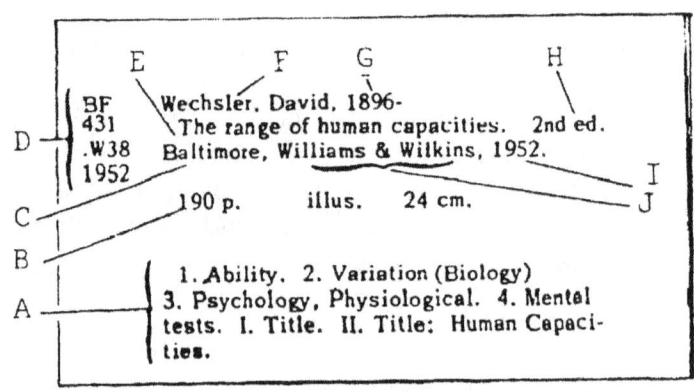

Sample Answer:

0. F

1. Date book was published.

2. Number of pages in book.

3. Title.

4. Place of publication.

5. Call number.

6. Year author was born

7. Edition.

8. Publisher.

9. Other headings under which cards for this book may be found.

Questions 10-13.

DIRECTIONS: Select the letter preceding the word or phrase which completes each of the following statements correctly.

10. The library's title card for the book THE LATE GEORGE APLEY can be found by looking in the card catalog under   10.____

    A. Apley, George   B. The   C. Late   D. George   E. Apley

11. A catalog card for a book by John F. Kennedy would be found in the drawer labelled   11.____

    A. JEFFERSON-JOHNSON,ROY
    B. PRESCOTT-PRICELESS
    C. KIERNAN-KLAY
    D. U.S.PRESIDENT-U.S.SOCIAL SECURITY
    E. KENNEBEC-KIERKEGAARD

12. The title cards for these three periodicals would be found in the card catalog arranged in which of the following orders: 12.____

    A. NEW YORKER, NEWSWEEK, NEW YORK TIMES MAGAZINE
    B. NEWSWEEK, NEW YORKER, NEW YORK TIMES MAGAZINE
    C. NEW YORK TIMES MAGAZINE, NEW YORKER, NEWSWEEK
    D. NEW YORKER, NEW YORK TIMES MAGAZINE, NEWSWEEK
    E. NEWSWEEK, NEW YORK TIMES MAGAZINE, NEW YORKER

13. A card for a copy of the U.N.Charter would be found in the catalog drawer marked   13.____

    A. TWENTIETH-UNAMUNO
    B. UNITED MINE WORKERS-UNITED SHOE MACHINERY
    C. U.S.BUREAU-U.S. CONGRESS
    D. U.S.SOCIAL POLICY-UNIVERSITAS
    E. CHANCEL-CIARDI

II. UNDERSTANDING ENTRIES IN A PERIODICAL INDEX

Questions 14-25.

DIRECTIONS: The following items are excerpts from THE READERS' GUIDE TO PERIODICAL LITERATURE. Identify each lettered section of the entries by placing the correct letters in the spaces.(There are more letters than spaces, so some of the letters will not be used.)

```
              V
A    UNITED NATIONS
      Ambassador Goldberg holds news conference at          H         Security Council
      New York; transcript of conference,                     Security Council urged to respond to
B     July 28, 1965; with questions and answers.              challenge in southeast Asia; letter,
      A. J. Goldberg. Dept. State Bul 53:272+         U    M  July 30, 1965. A. J. Goldberg. Dept
C     Ag 16 '65                                       T      State Bul 53:278-80+  Ag 16, '65
      U.N. out of its teens. I.D. Talmadge. il Sr Schol  S      L    •I    J   K
E     87:16-17+  S 16 '65
D     Whatever became of the United Nations?          Q
      America 113:235  S 4 '65
       F   R
              Charter                                 P
      Up-dating the pre-atomic United Nations; address,
      June 20, 1965. C.P. Romulo. Vital Speeches
      31:658-61 Ag 15 '65; Excerpts. Sat R 48:34-5+  O
      Jl 24 '65            N
                       G
```

14. Title of magazine containing a transcript of a news con-conference held by U.N. Ambassador Arthur Goldberg. 14.___

15. Magazine in which the full text of C.P. Romulo's address on the U.N. appears. 15.___

16. Author of an article titled U.N. OUT OF ITS TEENS. 16.___

17. Date on which Ambassador Goldberg wrote a letter urging the Security Council to respond to the challenge of southeast Asia. 17.___

18. Title of an article for which no author is listed. 18.___

19. Date of the SATURDAY REVIEW issue which contains excerptsl of a speech called "Up-Dating the Pre-Atomic United Nations." 19.___

20. Pages in the DEPARTMENT OF STATE BULLETIN on which Ambassador Goldberg's letter appears. 20.___

21. Symbol indicating that the letter is continued on a later page. 21.___

22. Volume number of the magazine in which the article by I.D. Talmadge is printed. 22.___

23. Symbols meaning September 16, 1965. 23.___

24. The general subject heading under which all five articles are listed. 24.___

25. A subject heading subdivision. 25.___

Questions 26-27.

DIRECTIONS: Select the letter preceding the phrase which completes each of the following statements correctly.

26. To determine whether or not the library has THE MAGAZINE OF AMERICAN HISTORY, check in 26.___

   A. the list of magazine titles in the front of THE READERS' GUIDE TO PERIODICAL LITERATURE
   B. the library's card catalog

C. Ulrich's GUIDE TO PERIODICALS
D. SATURDAY REVIEW
E. THE LIBRARY JOURNAL

27. THE READERS' GUIDE is a good place to look for material on the Job Corps because it   27.____

    A. indexes only the best books and magazines in each field
    B. is a guide to articles on many subjects appearing in all of the library's periodicals
    C. indexes recent discussions on the subject in many magazines
    D. specializes in official government information
    E. does all of the above

III. IDENTIFYING LIBRARY TERMS

Questions 28-32.

DIRECTIONS: Match the correct definitions with these terms by placing the correct letters in the blanks. (Some of the letters will not be used.)

28. Bibliography

    A. Word or phrase printed in A. Word or phrase printed in log to indicate the major log to indicate the major   28.____

29. Anthology

    B. Brief written summary of the major ideas presented in an article or book   29.____

30. Index

    C. List of books and/or articles on one subject or by one author   30.____

31. Abstract

    D. Collection of selections from the writings of one or several authors   31.____

32. Subject heading

    E. Written account of a person's life   32.____

    F. Alphabetical list of subjects with the pages on which they are to be found in a book or periodical

    G. Subordinate, usually explanatory title, additional to the main title and usually printed below it

IV. FINDING A BOOK BY ITS CALL NUMBER

Questions 33-38.

DIRECTIONS: The Library of Congress classification system call numbers shown below are arranged in order, just as the books bearing those call numbers would be arranged on the shelves. To show where other call numbers would be located, select the letter of the CORRECT ANSWER.

A.	B.	C.	D.	E.	F.	G.	H.	I.	J.	K.
PS 201 .L67 1961	PS 201 .M44	PS 208 .B87 1944	PS 351 .D7	PS 351 .D77	PS 3513 .A2	PS 3515 .D72	PS 3515.3 A66	PS 3526 .N21	PS 3526.17 P2	PS 3526.37 A10

		L.	M.	N.		
		PS 3526.37 C20	PS 3526.37 C37	PT 1 .R2		

33. A book with the call number PS
    201
    .L67

   A. Before A B. Between A & B C. Between B & C
   D. Between C & D E. Between D & E

34. A book with the call number PS
    208
    .B87
    1944a

   A. Between A & B B. Between C & D C. Between B & C
   D. Between C & D E. Between D & E

35. A book with the call number PS
    351
    D8

   A. Between C & D B. Between D & E C. Between E & F
   D. Between F & G E. Between G & H

36. A book with the call number PS
    3526.3
    M53

   A. Between L & M B. Between J & K C. Between K & L
   D. Between M & O E. Between O & P

37. A book with the call number PS
    3526.37
    C205

   A. Between L & M B. Between N & O C. Between M & N
   D. Between O & P E. Between P & Q

38. A book with the call number PS
    3526.37
    C3

   A. Between M & N B. Between L & M C. Between N & O
   D. Between O & P E. Between P & Q

V. General

Questions 39-40.

DIRECTIONS: Each question or incomplete statement is followed by several suggested answers or completions. Select the one that BEST answers the question or completes the statement. *PRINT THE LETTER OF THE CORRECT ANSWER IN TEE SPACE AT THE RIGHT.*

39. When it is finished (in 610 volumes), the _____ will be the MOST monumental national bibliography in the world. 39.____

    A. UNION LIST OF SERIALS IN LIBRARIES OF THE UNITED STATES AND CANADA
    B. UNITED STATES CATALOG
    C. READERS' GUIDE TO PERIODICAL LITERATURE
    D. NATIONAL UNION CATALOG

40. For those who wish to investigate the publishing companies and the people who control them, to locate the date a company was founded, who owned it, when it changed hands, what firm succeeded it, and other information of a similar nature, the periodical _____ is clearly invaluable. 40.____

    A. PUBLISHERS' TRADE LIST ANNUAL (PTLA)
    B. CUMULATIVE BOOK INDEX
    C. AMERICAN BOOKTRADE DIRECTORY
    D. PUBLISHERS WEEKLY

KEY (CORRECT ANSWERS)

1. I
2. B
3. E
4. C
5. D
6. G
7. H
8. J
9. A
10. C - The first word of the title which is not an article.
11. E - Every book in the library is listed in the card catalog under the author's name. (Warning: The "author" may be a society, a university, or some other institution.)
12. C - A title is alphabetized word-by-word; therefore, "New" comes before "Newsweek," "New York" before "New Yorker."
13. B - The United Nations, not an individual, is the author of this work.
14. T 16. Q 18. D 20. J 22. E 24. A 26. B 28. C 30. F 32. A
15. O 17. M 19. N 21. K 23. R 25. P/H 27. C 29. D 31. B
33. A - When two call numbers are identical except that one has a year or some other figure added at its end, the shorter call numbers comes first.
34. B
35. C - The numbers which follow a. are regarded as decimals; therefore, .D77 precedes .D8.
36. B - 3526.3 precedes 3526.37
37. A - .C20 precedes .C205
38. B - .C3 precedes .C37 (Read the call number line-by-line, and put a J before a P, before a PB, etc. Put a lower number before a greater one.)
39. D
40. D